C000240714

Stride Inside The Villa

Steve Stride

with

Rob Bishop

Sports Projects

•

First published in Great Britain in 1997 by
SPORTS PROJECTS LTD
188 Lightwoods Hill, Smethwick, Warley, West Midlands B67 5EH

•

ISBN 0 946866 40 6

•

•

A catalogue record for this book is available from the British Library

•

Printed in Great Britain

Contents

Foreword by Tom Watt

Four years ago, research for my second book took me to Villa Park. Not that it was my first visit, or that I needed an excuse. The place is one of English football's great stages, and I've been going there for the best part of 30 years. I've been to Cup replays, semi-finals, Villa v Arsenal clashes. I even got a game on the pitch once, not for the Gunners, but for the once-mighty Walford Boys Club, *Eastenders'* charity football XI.

I say "once-mighty" because the team has long disbanded. Mighty we were, though. On the particular Sunday morning in question, we tonked an all-star team, including Johnny Dixon, Dave Watson, Frank McLintock and Gordon Hill, 5-0.

That splendid occasion also offered a glimpse behind the scenes at a great football club, and I'm honoured that I've been made welcome at Villa Park ever since.

If you've spent any time at all around professional football, you'll know there's usually just one person at a club who has any idea of everything that's going on. The players, the manager, the chairman all have separate agendas, and will often keep their plans to themselves.

The club secretary, though, is different. Every piece of paper, every phone conversation in the life of Anytown FC will find its way through the secretary's office – contracts, fixtures, medical reports, FA directives, Board minutes, Press inquiries, the lot.

The secretary also needs to be privy to everybody else's secrets, which explains why he can usually help with the questions no-one else can answer.

What makes Steve Stride tick is that he exemplifies, in many ways, the character of the club he works for. Villa are a big club, no question, but there's a feeling around the place, too, that reminds you of a little local club – a lack of pretence, staff who are fans as well as employees, and a reassurance that loyalty counts for something at Villa Park.

Steve watched Villa from the Holte End as a kid. Standing on that massive terrace, it seems, he vowed never to grow up. It's a great story – the young supporter who gets his foot in the door, manages to keep it there and, after a working life devoted to the club, finds himself elected to the Board. It seemed an ideal story to kick off my book, *A Passion for the Game.*

I got to know Steve after my legendary appearance on the Villa Park pitch, and he invited me back when Arsenal played there. Even better, during runs in shows at the Rep and Alex theatres, I found Steve's office the perfect place for a coffee and chinwag about football.

Birmingham is an under-rated city and Villa, away from the fashionable spotlights cast on London and Manchester, has often been an under-rated club. My book, though, was going to be about the real world, and I hoped Steve would be prepared to help.

I wasn't disappointed. Introductions were furnished throughout the club – to the then manager Ron Atkinson, commercial manager Abdul Rashid, stadium tour-guide Jack Watts, physio Jim Walker. That was just the start. Out came Steve's address book, and staff at clubs all over the country, having been primed by my secretary pal, were ready and willing to assist me.

It was the kind of help without which my book couldn't have been written. All the more curious, then, that when I came to the story I was particularly keen to include – Steve's own – he said he couldn't help me.

Now I know why Steve wouldn't let me try to put his story into words. Fair enough, it's always better getting these things first hand. So welcome to *Stride Inside The Villa*. If you're interested in life inside a top football club and fancy being taken behind the scenes of the professional game, I think you're going to enjoy what follows here.

Tom Watt

Introduction

June 12, 1997

Dear Dad,

You've probably heard all about it by now, but we signed Stan Collymore the other week for £7 million. Would you believe it? *Seven million quid!* I bet you never thought you'd see the day when your beloved Aston Villa would fork out that kind of money for a new player. But that's the way the game is now. If you want top quality, you have to pay astronomical prices.

As Collymore's transfer from Liverpool was going through, I could not help thinking how things have changed during the past quarter of a century. It's exactly 25 years today since I joined Villa and during my first week at the club we signed a new striker. Remember him? Alun Evans was his name. He also joined us from Liverpool, although he cost something like a hundred times less than *Stan-The-Man*. Then again, £72,500 was a tidy sum in 1972.

Even in those days, I seem to recall you thought we had paid over the odds for a new player, particularly as your own favourites had cost next to nothing by comparison. That wasn't the only thing troubling you, either. You weren't exactly overjoyed when I told you about my new employment. Despite your affection for Villa, you were convinced there was no future in working for a football club.

Still, it hasn't turned out too badly, has it? I was just an office boy when we signed Alun Evans. By the time Stan Collymore came along, I'd been secretary for 18 years and a club director for nearly two years. And what other job would have taken me all over the continent and to far flung corners of the world, all in the cause of Aston Villa FC?

I've met a fair sprinkling of famous people along the way, too. All right, maybe the idea of mingling with the likes of Mick Hucknall, Kate Bush, Rod Stewart, Robbie Williams and Nigel Kennedy doesn't exactly appeal to you. But you must have been impressed when I came face to face with Nelson Mandela. There we were, at Ellis Park, Johannesburg, when we were confronted by one of the most influential leaders in world history. I couldn't have been more nervous if I had been meeting the Queen, but Nelson was a smashing bloke. He just shook my hand and said: "It's an honour to meet you, sir."

Well, you can imagine how that felt. I was nearly as elated as when Villa won the League Championship, or the European Cup, or the League Cup. Not quite, though. Although I've never pulled on the claret-and-blue shirt (not for a proper match, anyway), it's been brilliant just being involved in some of the triumphs our teams have enjoyed over the years.

An FA Cup victory would have made my time at Villa Park even more special, but I'm still waiting for that one. As you keep reminding me, it's 40 years since Villa won the Cup, and I know you still have fond memories of when Johnny Dixon led his side around Wembley in a lap of honour.

The book I've written is about my own recollections of life with Aston Villa, so there isn't a great deal about the likes of Johnny and his pals, even though I pursued them like a schoolkid to get their autographs at last month's 1957 Cup Final reunion dinner.

You won't find much about the team's achievements on the pitch, either. The idea is to give an insight into what it's been like behind the scenes. Football may be a serious business, but it is packed with characters, and there have been plenty of laughs along the way. Hope you enjoy it.

THIS BOOK IS DEDICATED TO

MY WIFE CAROLYN,

CHILDREN LUCY, MATTHEW AND JACK, MY FAMILY,

AND IN MEMORY OF

DR DAVID TARGETT,

A TRUE FRIEND WHO WILL BE GREATLY MISSED.

Chapter One

Please, Mr Postman

I first noticed him out of the corner of my eye, just as I emerged from a melee of congratulations from jubilant team-mates. There was no mistaking the tall, slender frame, the studious facial expression, the hair slicked back from his forehead. He'd barely changed at all since I had admired him from the Holte End.

Except that Gordon Lee was no longer an Aston Villa full-back. He was watching the match in his new capacity as a scout for the club, seeking out fresh young talent on the playing fields of Birmingham. And I had just scored the once-in-a-lifetime goal which would ensure word got back to the right quarters, and provide my launchpad to a glittering career as a professional footballer.

Let me talk you through it. From my position of left-back, I had pushed forward to the half-way line to receive a pass from one of my Erdington and Saltley Schoolboy colleagues. The move had begun promisingly, but suddenly there were no options ahead of me because of close-marking opponents.

What to do? Simple. Like any player worth his salt, I improvised, taking a couple of steps forward before letting fly with a speculative 50-yard shot which flew past an astonished goalkeeper into the top corner of the net.

All right, so Pele and David Beckham have tried it since (although I seem to recall the Brazilian ace was narrowly off target with his effort in the 1970 World Cup). But how many footballers can claim to have scored from that distance?

The observant Lee could not fail to be impressed, I told myself. As soon as the game was over, he would be compiling the report which would persuade Aston Villa to sign me up as an apprentice and set me on the way to fame and fortune.

It was just a matter of time before the approach was made. Like the man in the song, our own Mr Postman was ordered to look every day to see if there was a letter in his bag for me. If there was, it certainly hadn't been posted at Villa Park.

Every time there was a knock at the door, too, I convinced myself it was a representative of the club, armed with the appropriate forms for me to sign.

A week passed, then two. Nothing. I wasn't the first youngster to act out the fantasy of taking the first step to soccer stardom, and at the end of that frustrating fortnight I came to my senses. At the age of 15, I finally and reluctantly accepted that however else I might earn my living, it wasn't going to be as a footballer.

If Gordon Lee had been impressed with my wonder goal – and as a fellow full-back he surely must have been – he clearly did not see sufficient potential in the rest of my game to warrant a recommendation to Villa manager Dick Taylor.

In hindsight, of course, you come to realise just how long the odds are against making the grade. A few years ago, I came across the programme from a schoolboy international I had watched on my first visit to Wembley. Looking through the names in the England team, it dawned on me that only one, Colin Suggett, had progressed to the game's top level.

The other names on that team sheet meant nothing to me, and in that sobering moment it dawned on me just how futile my schoolboy ambitions had been. If 10 players considered good enough to play for their country at the age of 15 were unable to reach the big time, what chance was there for someone who had never graduated beyond regional representative football?

Not that I was able to take such a logical view for those two weeks after Gordon Lee witnessed my sensational goal. I awoke every day with fresh, but ultimately false hope. When it finally became apparent that my super strike was not going to prompt a knock on the door or correspondence through the letter box from Villa, I was devastated. Then again, I've always been a bit of a romantic when it comes to football.

Whenever people ask me about the first Villa match I ever saw, for instance, I conjure up images of being perched on my dad's shoulders at Wembley in 1957, shouting myself hoarse at every Villa attack in the FA Cup Final against Manchester United. In my mind's eye, I can remember Peter McParland's two goals as if he had scored them yesterday, not to mention the unbelievable elation when Johnny Dixon held the cup aloft in front of thousands of cheering Brummies. That was something to savour for all time.

I wonder how many other Villa fans claim that wonderful occasion as the first match they ever saw? Like me, many of them might well have let their imagination run wild. The truth is, I don't have a clue about my "debut" as a supporter. Much as the fantasy appeals to me, I have to confess it wasn't the 1957 Cup Final.

Any recollections I have of Villa's glorious triumph four decades ago have been gleaned from reading about the event, or watching film footage of the great day. I can't even claim to have watched the Final on television, either. In 1957, my parents were among millions in this country who had not yet committed themselves to the nation's latest phenomenon. Nor was I glued to the radio, or wireless, as it was known in those days. At the age of six-and-a-half, I'm afraid, the fact that Aston Villa were involved in English football's showpiece match meant sweet FA to me.

It's far more likely that I was either being dragged around the shops by my mother, or playing in the back garden, oblivious to the fact that Aston Villa were in the process of winning the Cup for the seventh time in their history.

Even so, it wasn't too long afterwards that my affection for one of the country's greatest football clubs began to take root. Then, as now, devotion to a particular club is an essential aspect of school life for most boys, and St Mary and St Margaret's Junior School at Castle Bromwich was no exception.

If you were to walk into any Birmingham classroom today and ask the kids which team they follow, I'll wager there will be a strong lobby in favour of Manchester United, Liverpool, Newcastle United and Arsenal, with a few youngsters possibly even pledging their allegiance to the likes of AC Milan, Real Madrid and Barcelona, glamorous foreign clubs which have captured their imagination because of the ever-widening world of television, not to mention the welter of glossy football magazines aimed specifically at impressionable young fans.

It wasn't like that back in the late 1950s. Even if you owned a TV, there was no such thing as live football apart from the Cup Final, and the only publication of any note was *Charles Buchan's Football Monthly*, which was aimed at a more adult readership.

With no outside influences to tempt our loyalty, either to other parts of the country or the Continent, Brummie kids were restricted to a simple choice. Even West Bromwich Albion, whose ground is barely three miles from Villa Park, did not enter the equation. You either supported Aston Villa or Birmingham City. Mostly, your preference was determined by which part of the city you came from, although Castle Bromwich was one of those grey areas where loyalties were divided straight down the middle.

Right from the start, Villa were my team, probably because my dad had always been such a staunch supporter of the boys in claret and blue. Maybe I didn't go to Wembley in 1957, but myself and my pals played out hundreds of finals in our minds. St Mary and St Margaret's, a traditional village school, didn't have a proper team, but once the final bell of the academic day had rung, someone invariably produced a football which we dribbled all the way home before hastily changing into our playclothes for the big kick-off out in the street.

Woodford Avenue, Castle Bromwich, was the venue for countless Villa-Blues derbies between wide-eyed, eager eight-year-olds. We engaged in marathon matches which kicked off after tea had been wolfed down, and continued until it was too dark to see either your opponents or the ball.

Throughout the football season and well into the summer months – in the days before many of us had actually watched our heroes in action – we either spilled into the street or on to a nearby open space called The Green, to engage in games which were as fervent as any which took place at Villa Park or St Andrew's.

Most families didn't have a great deal of money, and I can't recall anyone who turned out for our games in the replica kit which is regarded almost as obligatory by youngsters today. There was no shortage of imagination among our happy crowd, however. We played league matches, cup ties, even the odd European Cup match, but the teams never varied. It was always Aston Villa against Birmingham City – and I always pretended to be Gerry Hitchens, the legendary centre-forward who scored 96 goals in 160 games before leaving Villa for Italian giants Inter Milan in 1961.

I hadn't seen Hitchens play when I first adopted him as my role model. The closest I had come to seeing a footballer in the flesh, in fact, was by taking a stroll to another part of the estate where I lived, and even then a sighting wasn't always guaranteed.

All the same, I took great delight in boasting to my schoolmates that George Allen lived only a few streets from me, even if he did play for Birmingham City. In case the name isn't familiar, Allen was a left-back who made over 100 appearances for Blues between 1952 and 1961, when he was transferred to Torquay.

All right, so he wasn't what you would describe as a superstar, but he was a professional footballer, and he lived nearby. It didn't matter that he played for Villa's deadliest rivals. As often as I could, I took a walk past his house, hoping and praying he would be out cleaning his car. I did spot him on a couple of occasions, and once plucked up the courage to ask for his autograph, which made me the envy of the Blues supporters in our class.

But when it came to comparing George with Gerry, it was no contest, and not just because Hitchens played for Villa. He was, quite simply, the local hero, the man everyone talked about, and I wanted to be like him – blond-haired, handsome and lethal in front of goal. A friend of mine, whose father ran a cafe near the Villa ground, managed to get me the great man's autograph, which I treasured for many years, even if the paper on which it was scrawled became crumpled and dog-eared from countless nights of being squashed under my pillow.

When I was older, my collection of Villa signatures grew considerably. During school holidays I would go along to the club's old training ground in Trinity Road and spend the whole day waiting for the players to emerge. George Graham and Charlie Aitken were two of my favourites by then, and I was delighted when both of them scrawled their names in my book.

There were numerous occasions, too, when I took a 20-minute walk to the newsagents' shop owned by another of my idols, Vic Crowe. The business of buying a bag of sweets always took an eternity as I stood there desperately hoping Crowe would appear on the other side of the counter. He never did.

While I came to admire a good many Villa stars, however, it's certainly true that your first hero leaves a lasting impression. Of all the players I have met down the years, and the figure runs into hundreds, nothing has filled me with more excitement than when I met Gerry Hitchens, just a couple of years before his untimely death in 1983. By then he had long since retired from the game, but when he returned to the club for a reunion of former players, the prospect of coming face to face with him reduced me a to a nervous wreck.

People often say that meeting your idol can shatter your illusions, but Gerry was the perfect gentleman, putting me immediately at ease with his courteous and charming manner.

Despite Gerry's appealing nature, I was as awestruck as I had been back in his playing days. Although dates and opponents escape my mind, images of those first few visits to Villa Park have never faded. While dad sat in the stands, my vantage point was the Holte End, then a vast open terrace. It may sound strange that a young boy should stand alone at a football match among thousands of strange faces, but this was a good many years before the hooligan element crept into the game.

The people who inhabited the Holte, and other parts of the ground for that matter, were mostly honest, working-class folk who headed for Villa Park on Saturday afternoons to unwind after a long, tiring week on the factory floor. Youngsters like me were always given preferential treatment, being allowed to weave our way through the masses of adult bodies until we reached our favourite viewing position near the wall behind the goal-line.

You could almost smell and taste the action from there, although I can't claim to have ever watched a full match in those early days. Standing just above pitch level on the terraces offered a perfect view of anything which happened in the Holte End goal-mouth, and you also had a fairly clear impression of attacking moves which built up from the half-way line towards our end of the ground.

Anything beyond that, quite frankly, was a blur. On the journey home, dad would often say something like: "Wasn't that a great third goal?" waiting eagerly for my enthusiastic reply. Sometimes I just stared back blankly, unable to either confirm his opinion or argue otherwise. He soon became accustomed to giving me a descriptive re-run of any goals scored at the Witton End.

That all changed in 1962, thanks partly to my efforts in the classroom but more importantly, I believe, because of my devotion to Aston Villa. Most kids are either winners or losers when it comes to examinations, but I had to be different. I managed a draw.

When I sat my 11-plus exam to determine the venue of my educational future, I was described as a borderline case. This strange intermediate situation, of having neither passed nor failed, meant I had to attend an interview to determine whether I was destined for secondary or grammar school.

Keen to impress, I had my hair cut, tidied myself up and was taken along by my mother to confront three gentlemen who would make the big decision about the establishment in which I was to continue the important process of gathering knowledge.

I am convinced it was neither my immaculate appearance, nor even the answers I provided to the panel's questions, which clinched my place at Coleshill Grammar School. As a good luck charm, I had pinned a small enamel Villa badge to the lapel of my school blazer, and the ploy paid unexpected dividends even before a serious question had been asked.

One of the interviewers spotted my badge, and for a couple of minutes or more, we chatted away happily about a subject which was far more important to me than English, Maths and History. Who was my favourite player? How long had I been going to Villa Park? What about the team's chances for the following season?

The prospect of facing this crucial interview had been more than a little daunting, but it was quickly turning out to be a highly-enjoyable experience. My nerves had all but disappeared, and I was starting to feel relaxed. If only questions of a similar nature had been presented on the 11-plus examination sheet, I would have sailed through with flying colours!

No doubt the interview eventually turned to matters of a more serious and important nature. After all, we couldn't sit there all day talking about Aston Villa, much as I would have liked to. But whatever else was said during the remainder of that selection session, I clearly came up with the correct answers, and was subsequently informed I was to attend Coleshill Grammar from the following September.

My parents, needless to say, were absolutely delighted – and so was

I when dad presented me with my reward for being such a clever boy. Not for me an encyclopaedia or a bound volume of the Classics. The book dad bought me measured barely four inches by three, but it contained precious sheets of paper which would admit me through Door H of the Trinity Road stand for the duration of the 1962-63 campaign. No longer would I have to settle for watching half a match from the Holte End. As a season ticket holder, I was now afforded a panoramic view of the whole pitch from seat 102 of row M.

This opened up a whole new world for me. The players were not in such close proximity as they had been in the Holte goal-mouth, but now I could appreciate the quality of their passing and ball control so much better. Wingers Harry Burrows and Jimmy McEwan were my new favourites in the wake of Hitchens' transfer to Italy, although Derek Dougan was undoubtedly the character of the team.

The towering Irish centre-forward had a rebellious nature, too. We were all stunned when he stepped out for a pre-season practice match between the *Probables* and the *Possibles* with his head shaved completely bald.

That sort of thing wouldn't turn a hair today, if you'll forgive the pun, but in the early 1960s it was quite astonishing. Doog, to be fair, was headstrong in more ways than one, even after his playing days were over. Years later, after he had got involved with a consortium which took over Wolverhampton Wanderers, I became embroiled in a heated discussion with him in the Villa Park boardroom over Wolves' ticket allocation for an FA Cup-tie.

I tried to explain that the number of places for visiting fans was restricted for every match, because we had to look after the interests of our own supporters, while Dougan claimed – rightly so, no doubt – that Wolves supporters could have filled their section of terracing four times over.

As the argument intensified, Doog became quite aggressive towards me, and I could see how he had terrorised defenders a few years earlier. Apart from being an unpleasant situation, it was also becoming very embarrassing, with other guests listening to every word which was uttered between the two of us.

Thankfully, help was at hand. Chairman Doug Ellis intervened, told Dougan he was not impressed with his behaviour, and requested him to leave. Doog stormed out, and to my knowledge has never since been invited into the boardroom.

Two decades earlier, however, Dougan was one of the players whose Villa Park exploits persuaded me that my future lay in the glamorous world of professional football. It didn't seem such an impossible dream, either.

In the year above me at grammar school was a lad called Alan Merrick, who went on to play for West Brom, and I was determined to follow a similar path, albeit with Villa Park instead of The Hawthorns, as the ultimate destination.

I captained the school team and also got myself fixed up with a club called Brookhill, who were named after the Brookhill pub in Alum Rock. Run by a fellow by the name of Bill Wilcox, they were one of the best-organised junior clubs in Birmingham, fielding five teams of various age groups every Saturday and Sunday.

Maybe they were connected to a pub, but Brookhill were run on a professional basis, with regular training sessions in midweek. They also attracted some excellent players. Graham Allner, later to make a name for himself as manager of Kidderminster Harriers, was in the team above mine.

At one stage we were even affiliated to Walsall FC, which enabled us to go to the old Fellows Park ground for treatment if we ever got injured. It was at Walsall that I met the former Villa trainer Ray Shaw, who was working for the Saddlers by then. Being able to go behind the scenes at a Football Club also gave me an even bigger appetite for the big time.

In addition, I was starting to make an impression on the school playing fields, my selection for the Erdington and Saltley representative side providing yet another step in the right direction.

By the time we reached under-15 level, several of the lads in the side fancied their chances of going on to bigger and better things, and the incentive was certainly there. The previous year, Erdington had won the prestigious English Schools Trophy, beating Chester-le-Street in front of a huge crowd at Villa Park, and we were determined to emulate their feat.

Sadly, that dream was shattered when we didn't even progress beyond the regional stages, losing 4-3 to local rivals South Birmingham. Their team wasn't a great deal better than ours, but one of their strikers was a different class to everyone else on the pitch, creating all sorts of problems for our defence and scoring a hat-trick. I subsequently discovered his name was Bob Latchford, who was to continue his prolific goalscoring with the likes of Birmingham City and Everton.

It wasn't long after Latchford's hat-trick for South Birmingham that I scored my famous goal from the half-way line (at least, that's the distance which is etched in my memory), the one which failed to stir Villa's watching scout into prompt action.

For some considerable time after giving up on my futile vigil, waiting for a letter or a knock at the door, I privately cursed Gordon Lee for having nothing to say on my behalf. Little could I have known that 18 years later, I would witness him having far too much to say for his own good...

Captain of Coleshill Grammar School in 1965 (the day I stopped growing!).

Chapter Two

From Rochdale With Rust

It was all too easy for me to identify with Aston Villa by the time I started going to away matches on a regular basis. We were both having a hard time.

Villa had plummeted to the old Third Division for the first time in their history, and I certainly wasn't travelling in style as I followed them all over the country. My job as an estimator at a local air-conditioning company was not only tedious, it didn't pay a fat lot, either.

While the team relaxed in their luxury coach, I chugged along in an old Austin A40 which cost £35 and had been gloriously resprayed in gold – the same colour as the rust underneath. My first car also had an ill-fitting latch, which meant that every so often – and always without warning – the bonnet would shoot up, completely blocking my view of the road.

I lost count of the times I had to brake sharply and get out of the car to force the bonnet back into place, wondering how many miles I would be able to cover before the next mishap. One trip home from Halifax on a cold November evening took me the best part of six hours as my temperamental bonnet reared its ugly head every 20 minutes or so. My temper was hardly improved, either, by the fact Villa had lost 2-1.

Whatever the faults of my old rust box, though, it was probably the best 35 quid I've ever spent. My A40 was golden in more ways than one. It enabled me to follow my favourite team to away matches on a regular basis, and I had some wonderful days out at unlikely places such as Rochdale, Reading and Rotherham.

Those two seasons in football's lower reaches also got Villa supporters back into the habit of following a winning team after the lean years which had seen our team relegated from the First Division and then the Second. Now we were the great Aston Villa, visiting the game's poor relations and giving them a helping hand – in a financial rather than football sense. While we headed home from most venues happy with the result, the home club directors were no doubt rubbing their hands at the receipts from what was invariably their biggest crowd of the season.

Not that memorable moments were restricted to away-days. There were also some pretty special occasions at Villa Park during the club's exile in Division Three. Like the day we beat fellow promotion candidates Bournemouth in front of over 48,000, a record attendance for that division which will surely never be bettered. Or the night a staggering 58,667 squeezed into the ground for the second leg of a League Cup semi-final against Manchester United.

That was, without question, the greatest game I've ever seen. Maybe it was sheer emotion, but beating the mighty Mancunians – Charlton, Law, Kidd and the rest – was something to savour. Many of us could barely believe that our favourites had managed to force a 1-1 draw in the first leg at Old Trafford (the best 20th birthday present I could have had), but when Brian Kidd gave United an early lead in the return match, there was little prospect of a giant-killing act.

But Andy Lochhead equalised in the second half, and after 72 minutes Pat McMahon scored with a spectacular header to sweep my heroes into the Final. All right, we lost 2-0 to Tottenham, but there was an enormous feeling of pride that Villa had emerged from the darkest days of their history to reach a Wembley Final, the club's first for 14 years. And, unlike the 1957 FA Cup Final, I didn't have to use my powers of imagination this time. I was actually there in 1971.

The following year brought promotion for Villa, who went up as champions with a record number of points, but while I cheered every goal and every victory, little did I realise just how the team's achievement would enhance my own career prospects.

A few months earlier I had written to Doug Ellis, asking for a job at Villa Park, but although the letter of reply was signed by the chairman, it amounted to no more than a standard rejection, informing me there were no administrative vacancies at the club. Then, to make matters worse, my employers Albert E. Shaw went out of business. The only saving grace was that I was kept on by the Receiver, so at least I wasn't out of work. At a time when I was celebrating Villa's success, my personal horizons were pretty limited. Basically I was going nowhere fast.

Then, right out of the blue, another envelope bearing the Aston Villa logo dropped through the letter box, and this time the contents were much more to my liking. Secretary Alan Bennett informed me that the club had just been promoted from the Third Division to the Second (as if I needed telling!), and as a result were taking on an extra member of staff for the following season. My earlier application had been kept on file, and would I like to go along for an interview?

I couldn't believe my luck, but I was more determined than I had ever been in my life that I was going to get the job. There was just one problem. Would my anxiety to impress lead to nerves which might result in me making a mess of the interview? I need not have worried.

Alan put me at ease by doing most of the talking as we sat in his office, telling me stories about his days at Chelsea and the Football Association, and the various trips abroad which life in football had brought him. He also made comments like "When you join us, you will find...", which prompted even a pessimist like me to believe I had a good chance of landing the job.

Then it was waiting time again, just as it had been after my wonderful display for Erdington and Saltley Schoolboys all those years earlier. Every morning, I rushed downstairs to see if a letter confirming my appointment was waiting for me. After a week had passed, I began to have my doubts. For the second time in my life, it looked like I was going to be let down by my favourite football club.

If I hadn't impressed Gordon Lee with my efforts on the pitch in 1966, however, it seems I made my mark in Alan Bennett's office in 1972. Ten days after the interview, that long-awaited letter came through the front door. The position of administrative assistant was mine if I wanted it.

My father, strangely enough, did not share my elation, even though he was the one who had nurtured my interest in Villa and had rewarded my achievement in getting to grammar school with a Trinity Road season ticket. To him, football was for recreation, not for work. I had failed him by not buckling down at school, and throwing away the chance of becoming a doctor or a barrister.

Despite being a lifelong Villa supporter, he couldn't see what future a job at a football club would hold for me. I was disappointed that he wasn't excited for me, but only one thing really mattered. I was off to work for the Villa.

Chapter Three

Taxman

Aston Villa made two new signings during the second week of June 1972. One cost them £72,500 (around £2m at today's transfer prices) and had established himself as a prolific goalscorer with his previous clubs, Wolverhampton Wanderers and Liverpool. The other arrived on a free transfer (around nothing at today's prices) and had failed to hit the target with either of his previous employers, H. Sutton and Albert E. Shaw.

If my appointment by Villa was significant for no other reason, I will always be able to claim I was recruited at the same time as Alun Evans, the blond-haired striker who was, at the time, one of the most expensive players ever signed by the club.

We had been brought in for the same reason, too – to help Villa cope with life back in the Second Division (today known as the First) after their humiliating experience of spending two seasons in Division Three.

It had been the first and only time in the distinguished history of the club that they had dropped below the Football League's top two sections, and the likes of Alun Evans and myself were brought in to ensure there would be no such repetition. All right, so I'm exaggerating.

The true situation was Evans was brought in to ensure there would be no such repetition. I was just a new addition to the office staff, employed to assist with the increasing workload of an understaffed administration.

Evans' importance to the club compared with my own was reflected in our wage packets. His salary was £60 per week, plus an annual lump sum of £1,000, and a further £500-a-year loyalty bonus. I received the princely sum of £23 a week. Not that I should complain. At £4,500 per anum Evans earned a basic salary, without bonuses, of four times my remuneration. Today, a similar scenario would see a new signing receiving nearer 40 times as much as a young member of staff. I did, however, have the distinction of beating Evans into Villa's history books. My starting date at Villa Park was June 12, but I subsequently discovered I had warranted a mention at a Board Meeting two weeks earlier, on May 30. Under the sub-heading *New Appointment*, the minutes read: "The secretary reported that he had appointed Mr S. Stride as Administrative Assistant as from the 12th of June, at a salary of £1200 per annum."

Even our YTS youngsters would laugh at such a wage in the 1990s, but in 1972 it wasn't such a bad figure, particularly for a newcomer with absolutely no experience of working for a football club. To put things in perspective, you could buy a season ticket for the best seat at Villa Park for £17, match day seats cost 90p and 70p, and a programme would set you back all of 7p, so I wasn't about to start complaining about receiving £23 a week for doing something I had always wanted. I was due to start at 9am on that first morning, but I presented myself in my best suit at 8.30am, raring to go and willing to tackle any duties presented to me.

It was perhaps as well, because Villa had an administrative staff of just seven when I joined – secretary Alan Bennett, commercial manager Eric Woodward, Pam Tabberner and Len Latham in the ticket office, Pam Milliard on the switchboard, plus two secretaries who had strong connections with past and future Villa players. Alan Bennett's secretary was Jill Moss, daughter of Amos Moss, who had made over 100 appearances for the club just after the War, while Heather Watson worked for both Eric Woodward and manager Vic Crowe. Her maiden name may not be familiar, but Heather later became Mrs Brian Little.

My appointment took the office staff complement to a grand total of eight (today, the figure is more than 30), and it was perhaps as well I set my stall out from that first day to be a workaholic. Basically, there was no choice. But I didn't mind one bit. During those whirlwind first few weeks I was continually coming into contact with people like Bruce Rioch, Ian Ross, Chico Hamilton and Charlie Aitken, players I had idolised from the Trinity Road stand and the terraces of Halifax and Rochdale only a few months earlier.

Now, I was not only meeting them face to face and passing the time of day with them, I even had access to their payslips. For me, doing a job had always been a necessary evil. It was something I had done purely so I could afford to follow Villa around the country, but this was much, much different. Now I was employed by my favourite club, it wasn't so much a job, but a hobby for which I was actually paid at the end of each week. I couldn't wait to get to work in the morning, and I never really wanted to go home at night. And even when I did force myself to leave the Villa Park offices, I usually carried home a bundle of paperwork which often kept me up past midnight. Never mind league tables, I used to spend hours most evenings studying Income Tax tables so I could calculate deductions from the salaries of Messrs Rioch, Hamilton, Ross and the rest of the players.

Apart from the wages of the playing staff, I was also responsible for the groundsmen, maintenance staff, cleaners, stewards, turnstile operators and anyone else employed by Villa on a casual basis. Then there was all the club's banking and book-keeping (all hand written by Yours Truly, this was before the dawn of the *Computer Age*), plus regular stints in the Ticket Office whenever the need arose. With Pam Tabberner and Len Latham the only two regular members of staff in there, the rest of us would often have to drop everything and spend days coping with the demands of Cup-ties and other big matches, which usually resulted in even more work being taken home. No-one minded, though. We were one happy family, doing our best for the Villa cause, and being the new boy made me more enthusiastic than anyone. I was so concerned about the welfare of the club that although we had a nightwatchman, I frequently used to go around the whole ground before leaving, making sure every door and gate was locked.

If I possessed a keen attitude right from the outset, however, the machinations of Aston Villa FC went right over my head in those early days. The first few months were like a whirlwind as I tried to comprehend the policies and politics of one of the country's leading football clubs, which is how Villa have always regarded themselves, even during seasons spent outside the top flight. Until my appointment, Villa Park had been somewhere to watch a football match and forget the troubles of the working week. Now, it was at the very heart of my working week.

I soon discovered, too, that Villa Park could be utilised for more than just 90 minutes of football. Two weeks and one day after my arrival, the club hosted the Jack Solomons-Alex Griffiths promotion of the British Heavyweight Boxing Championship between Jack Bodell and Danny McAlinden, with the ring situated on the centre circle, and the rest of the playing surface converted into a ringside seating area.

A fight closer to home was the famous Boardroom Battle which raged through August and September that year, when Doug Ellis was the subject of a vote of No Confidence, and was temporarily ousted as chairman by Jim Hartley. The issue was finally resolved at an EGM on September 25, when a stage was erected on the pitch, and the Witton Lane stand was packed with shareholders who voiced their opinions as loudly as they would have done at a Villa home match. I found the whole business fascinating, although I was much too inexperienced in the job to fully understand all the implications.

The upshot of that vociferous meeting was that Jim Hartley, Bob Mackay and Dick Greenhalgh were removed from the Board, Harry

Kartz and Eric Houghton were elected new members, and Mr Ellis was re-instated to the chair. Not that any of this upheaval meant a great deal to me. I just looked on in bewilderment, intrigued at what was happening in the Boardroom, but relieved that it didn't affect my position. I was like a child in a toyshop, getting more and more involved in the day-to-day running of the club which meant everything to me. What's more, I was getting 23 quid a week for the privilege. Alun Evans may have made all the headlines when he signed for Villa that second week of June, 1972, but without ever pulling on a claret-and-blue shirt, I reckon I got a far bigger kick out of joining the club.

Just imagine how I felt when I was invited on to the team coach for an early season match at Burnley as Alan Bennett's assistant. Travelling with the players, and enjoying a pre-match meal with them, gave me a tremendous thrill, although I did my best to look nonchalant about it all. Then, on arriving at Turf Moor, I had to push my way through crowds of Villa supporters before watching the game from the Directors' Box alongside Burnley's famous chairman Bob Lord and the actor Peter Adamson, who played the part of Len Fairclough in the television soap opera *Coronation Street*. And Alun Evans wasn't even on the substitutes' bench!

Chapter Four

Across The Universe

Ask any of Villa's players how they felt about winning the League Championship and qualifying for the European Cup for the first time in the club's history, and they will no doubt respond with that popular football cliché about being *over the moon*. When we launched our triumphant Euro campaign of 1981-82, I wasn't so much over the moon – I thought we had landed on it.

Neil Armstrong may have achieved the feat for the first time 12 years earlier, but as our Aer Lingus charter flight approached Reykjavik airport on Monday September 28, 1981, we noticed that the whole place was covered in black dust, just like the lunar landscape Armstrong and his American astronaut pals had described. My first venture into European competition as club secretary had widened my geographical horizons even before we touched down. I'd read at school that Iceland was a strange country, but now I could see for myself.

Thankfully, first impressions were misleading, even if I wouldn't particularly recommend Iceland for a holiday. It was bitterly cold, and the tiny ground of FC Valur, our first round opponents, was situated right next to a fish factory. Believe me, the stench was so bad it made us all feel sick. How our players got through that second leg without vomiting on the pitch, I'll never know.

Putting aside the fact it was cold and smelly, however, the welcome from our Valur hosts could not have been warmer. They were only a small club (the attendance for that second leg tie was just 3,500), but their officials couldn't do enough to ensure that we enjoyed our stay. On our first night, we were taken on a tour of the town, followed by a visit to a nightclub, where I was amazed to see some of our players sneaking sheepishly away as we arrived. Nothing was ever said publicly about their indiscretion, but I gather they didn't get away with it. Roy McLaren, our assistant manager at the time, told me a few years later he was waiting for them when they returned to the hotel, and gave them a right old dressing down.

If some of the players stepped out of line on that first evening, it was our physio Jim Williams who found himself in the doghouse the following day. Our hosts, clearly determined to impress us, had hired a small plane to give us an aerial tour. As this was my first European away match as club secretary, I declined the offer, deciding I should stay with the team in case any administrative problems cropped up. But Jim, eager to expand his knowledge, accepted the invitation.

Manager Ron Saunders was not altogether happy about this, and stressed to Jim before he left: "Make sure you are back by 4 o'clock. That's when we go to the stadium for training." When Williams did not return at the appointed time, Saunders was quietly seething, but after the training session had been completed without any mishaps, he decided to exact his revenge on our high-flying physio.

Back at the hotel, the players strapped together the legs of Mark Jones, one of our young reserves, and poured brandy over him. When Williams returned he was told the youngster had broken both his legs in a training accident, and was rushed into the room where Jones was lying in apparent agony. The lad played his part brilliantly, screaming at the top of his voice as soon as Williams tried to touch his legs. Then panic set in. Our physio smelled the brandy, and asked nervously: "Has he been drinking?"

Quick as a flash, Saunders piped up: "Of course he's been drinking, it was the only way we could kill the pain!" As Williams' face froze in horror, it was all too much for everyone else. We all collapsed in fits of laughter that our physio had been taken in by Jones's mock injury, and Williams breathed an enormous sigh of relief. The incident had the desired effect, though. He never missed another training session.

By the time Gary Shaw scored twice to give us a 2-0 win over Valur, and a comfortable 7-0 aggregate, I was starting to feel at ease with the business of European ties. But that certainly hadn't been the case before the first leg at Villa Park two weeks earlier. For me, that was the big test, because the UEFA ruling was that home clubs should always make all the arrangements for their visitors. Other club officials get involved to some extent, but ultimately the buck stops with the secretary, and this was new ground for me.

Determined to do things properly and as efficiently as possible, I travelled to Merseyside and spent a couple of hours in the company of my Liverpool counterpart Peter Robinson, who had organised so many European ties for the Anfield club that the whole procedure had become second nature to him. Peter explained all the arrangements which needed to be made, outlined the protocol required when dealing with foreign opposition, warned me about a few possible pitfalls and generally offered a crash course on the whole issue.

He did, however, fail to mention one potential pitfall, probably because it was something he had never come across. What do you do when you are trying to book accommodation for a party of 30 players and officials from a visiting club, and there isn't a hotel room to be found anywhere in Birmingham? An Autumn Fair was taking place at the nearby National Exhibition Centre, and every hotel, both in the city centre and outlying areas, was fully booked throughout September.

After endless hours on the phone, we eventually managed to book the rooms we required at the Post House in Stoke-on-Trent, 50 miles north of Birmingham. I hate to think what the reaction might have been had we informed the likes of Juventus, Barcelona or Inter Milan, but the Icelandic officials accepted the situation without complaint –

possibly because I exaggerated slightly by saying the journey from the hotel to Villa Park was no more than half-an-hour. Well, it would be with a Formula One car on a clear motorway!

I must have decided to test the theory once our guests had arrived. Feeling guilty that the Valur party were staying so far away, we travelled to Stoke for the customary dinner the night before the game – and I was stopped on the M6 on the return journey by a policeman who informed me I had been driving at 90mph.

But a speeding fine wasn't all I had to show for my first European match as secretary. I also made two very good friends in Baldvin Jonson and Haldor Einersson, who were in charge of Valur's travel plans. My association with these gentlemen continued long after that opening round tie. Haldor was a clothing manufacturer, whose company Henson later became our shirt manufacturers, while I'm still in regular contact with Baldvin. We probably got on so well because alcoholic beer is banned in Iceland, and I was able to sneak a few cans of duty-free beer through the customs for them when we went to Valur for the return match.

The prospect of slipping anything illegal through the Green Channel was something I wouldn't even have contemplated on our next venture. Things may have changed since the fall of the Berlin Wall, but in those days, you didn't dare step out of line when visiting Eastern Europe.

That was stressed to me in no uncertain terms by Ken Smailes, secretary of Nottingham Forest, when I approached him for guidance ahead of our second round tie against Dynamo Berlin. We had to go behind the Iron Curtain for the first leg, and the last thing we wanted was to upset our Communist hosts.

Forest had played Dynamo two years earlier on their way to a second consecutive European Cup triumph, and Ken was able to tell me everything Villa would need to know about East Berlin. "As you go through Passport Control," he told me, "you will notice there are mirrors everywhere, even on the floor. That's to make sure no-one slips out of the country." With Ken's piece of information still ringing in my ears, I was hesitant about purchasing anything from the duty-free shop on the outward journey, let alone any items to which the German Democratic Republic police may have taken exception.

My impressions of East Berlin were rather less than favourable. Everywhere you turned, you were left with depressing images of poverty and greyness, and the lightbulbs seemed to generate no more than 30 watts. Still, it was educational to say the least, and once again I was glad of the opportunity to visit a place I would never have dreamed of as a holiday destination.

We were taken to see Hitler's Bunker, and our hotel was only a short distance from the Brandenburg Gate, so a few of us took a stroll to view one of Europe's most famous landmarks. You could see right into West Berlin from there, and I felt desperately sorry for the East Germans who gazed across to the west, knowing that any attempt to cross the border would end with a bullet in the back from the guards who patrolled the "wall".

If Berlin was bleak, however, our players certainly lit up the JahnSportspark stadium with a performance which earned us not only a 2-1 win but two crucial away goals which ultimately ensured our passage to the quarter-finals after Dynamo had won the second leg 1-0 at Villa Park. The match in Berlin was memorable for a penalty save by Jimmy Rimmer and even more so for the second of Tony Morley's brace of goals, when he made an electrifying run from one penalty area to the other before firing home the winner. One or two of Villa's other younger players often felt victimised by manager Ron Saunders, and Tony took great delight in sticking two fingers up to the boss as he ran back past the dug-out. Ron was a strict disciplinarian, but I seem to recall Morley got away with that particular show of dissent!

Our eventual away goals victory meant we had created a small piece of football history. With holders Liverpool also getting through, it was the first time two English clubs had reached the last eight of the European Cup since the competition's inception in 1955-56, the other six qualifiers being Anderlecht, Bayern Munich, Red Star Belgrade, CSKA Sofia, Craiova of Romania and the team we were paired with when the draw took place in Zurich on December 11 – Dynamo Kiev. Once again, we had to cross the dreaded Iron Curtain, this time into deepest Russia.

By the time we flew out for the first leg the following March, Ron Saunders, the man who had masterminded Villa's Championship success the previous season, had resigned and been replaced by his assistant Tony Barton. Not long afterwards, Saunders took charge of our rivals Birmingham City, and I reckon he decided that joining the old enemy across the city was preferable to having another taste of Communism. He was right, too. If East Berlin had been dull and depressing, the trip to Russia was a total nightmare.

For starters, we were told we wouldn't actually be playing in Kiev because temperatures of minus eight degrees had left the pitch frozen solid, with no prospect of a thaw. A phone call from the Soviet Union informed me that the game would take place either in Tashkent on the Chinese border, or at Sevastopol on the Black Sea. If this was Dynamo's version of Russian Roulette, it certainly had the desired effect, putting everyone at Villa Park on edge as we wondered just where we would be playing the first leg, and when we could go ahead with travel arrangements.

The cloak-and-dagger situation showed no sign of easing even when a deputation from Dynamo arrived in Birmingham to watch our lads in action, and told us it might be the day of the match before the venue was known. Once again, uncertain weather prospects were offered as the reason for the delay, and we had to resort to UEFA to get a firm ruling. On February 19, the Russians were ordered by the European football's governing body that they had until the following Monday to arrange the venue.

It was the Tuesday before we learned our destination, not that we were much the wiser for knowing. The first leg was scheduled for the Lokomotive Stadium in a place called Simferopol, 300 miles south of

Kiev, in the Crimea. But while the name didn't ring any bells, at least we could finally get down to making plans for the 2,000-mile flight.

We were determined to leave nothing to chance, either. If you've ever been to Russia, or many other Eastern European countries for that matter, you will know that food hygiene is not all it should be. There had been plenty of stories in the past about English footballers going down with stomach bugs before important matches in that part of the world, so the answer was simple. We took our own chef. When our plane took off from Birmingham airport on Monday, March 1, the players and officials were accompanied by 150 steaks, 12 dozen eggs and 112lb of potatoes, plus cereals, bread, tea and coffee.

When we saw our hotel, everyone was relieved at the decision to go "self-catering". Situated in a dismal industrial area, it was sparsely furnished and clearly intended for commercial travellers rather than tourists. In this country, it would have struggled to warrant a one-star rating. Down the years, the Russians have been notorious for making life as difficult as possible for visiting teams, and they certainly lived up to their reputation on this occasion. The tiny beds didn't exactly enhance a good night's sleep, either. Central defender Ken McNaught, at 6ft 2in one of the tallest players in the squad, took one look at his room and declared: "If you think I'm sleeping in that bed, you must be ***** joking!"

Sadly, there was no alternative, for Ken or any of us, but we were determined not to let our grim surroundings deflect the team from the task in hand. Once everyone had settled in, we all gathered in the hotel dining room for a typical English meal of steak and chips, content in the knowledge that at least the Russians would not be able to inflict any unsavoury local delicacies upon us. We should have known better. One of the skips containing our provisions had not been unlocked, so the hotel provided the bread to accompany that first evening meal. I will never forget the look on midfielder Gordon Cowans' face as he broke open his bread roll and a huge cockroach crawled out! All of these problems – the change of venue, the substandard accommodation and the poor hygiene – were highlighted by chairman Harry Kartz when he addressed our Dynamo Kiev hosts at the official banquet before the match. While Kartz pulled no punches, however, our interpreter, Liverpool University lecturer George Scanlon, decided that diplomacy was a better course to follow. I suspect the chairman's scathing remarks about the treatment we had received were toned down by the time they reached Russian ears, because there was no sign of animosity. Or perhaps the Kiev committee men couldn't have cared less about our discomfort as long as it helped them to get the result they wanted.

Happily, that didn't happen. Our lads displayed tremendous resilience to force a goalless draw before goals from Gary Shaw (later voted European Young Player of the Year) and Ken McNaught gave us a 2-0 scoreline in the return match a fortnight later. We had emerged from arguably the most daunting European tie the Villa have ever encountered, and were through to the last four of Europe's premier competition.

After the long hauls of the first three rounds, the semi-final was almost like a derby clash, involving only a short journey to Belgium to take on Anderlecht. Little could we have realised that after all the red tape surrounding the Russian excursion, we would face a similar problem just across the channel – this time, quite literally.

Anderlecht are one of the most experienced clubs in Europe, but when I made the customary visit to their ground before the tie, I was appalled by their security measures, or rather, lack of any. Football hooliganism was still a major problem, both in this country and on the Continent, but Anderlecht's method of segregating rival fans was a piece of red tape. Quite frankly, it was pathetic, particularly when we were talking about a capacity crowd at the second leg of a European Cup semi-final. Although we held on for a goalless draw, going through by virtue of Tony Morley's first leg goal, our elation at reaching the final was dampened by crowd disturbances and a pitch invasion. We watched in dismay as the trouble, apparently started by a British soldier based in Germany, unfolded before our eyes, and the game was held up for six minutes while police attempted to restore order.

At the end, after our lads had valiantly held on for a goalless draw which gave us a 1-0 aggregate victory, emotions were mixed, to say the least. Allan Evans described it as his greatest night in football, having overcome one of the best teams on the Continent to reach the European Cup Final, but for many of us, the delight was tinged by apprehension at the action we may face over the crowd disturbances.

As we expected, UEFA held a tribunal to get to the bottom of the matter, and I accompanied Denis Howell, the MP for Small Heath, to Zurich to present our case. Denis is a keen Villa supporter, but it was his persuasive powers, honed during his years as Minister for Sport and other political posts, which helped us to escape with a relatively light punishment.

Although we were heavily fined and ordered to play our next home European tie behind closed doors, financial loss was the least of our worries. If Anderlecht had got their way, our Final place would have been in jeopardy, because the Belgians wanted the second leg replayed, arguing that they were about to score when fans invaded the pitch.

I feared the worst, too, because I certainly couldn't recall the state of play when the match was stopped. From the moment we entered the room for that hearing in Zurich, I felt we were up against it. English clubs always seem to have been more heavily punished than their counterparts across Europe for the misbehaviour of supporters, and I had the distinct impression the knives were out for us as that meeting progressed.

Then Denis, bless him, came up with a simple question which knocked the wind out of Anderlecht's sails and ensured that Aston Villa would not have to endure a tense second leg re-run for the right to face German giants Bayern Munich in the Final.

Our opponents' call for a replay was based on their insistence that they had been denied a goal by fans running on to the pitch. Denis, a former first class referee, stopped them in their tracks. Addressing the commission in a calm, methodical manner, he said: "Can I ask you where the referee restarted the match after the invasion?"

Those few words kicked the Anderlecht case right out of court. When the gentlemen of the panel checked, the answer was that the game had resumed just inside our own half – and the Belgians could hardly argue they were about to break through our rock-solid defence from there. The fine imposed on us and the behind-closed-doors directive ultimately seemed little more than a rap across the knuckles, compared with what we stood to lose in that room – and what we would surely have lost, but for the astute Mr Howell.

There was an immense feeling of relief that our Final place had not been jeopardised, but the unsavoury events in Belgium had put us on our guard against a possible repetition when we played Bayern in Rotterdam's Feyenoord Stadium at the end of May.

Andelecht's segregation might have been described as a joke, had the consequences not been quite so serious. While our Final place remained unaffected, we still had the behind-closed-doors punishment hanging over our heads. The last thing anyone wanted was further trouble and a lengthy ban from European competition, and I'm sure UEFA would have had no hesitation in imposing such a sentence had there been crowd problems at the stadium known in Holland as De Kuip – "*The Tub*".

With that very much to the forefront of our minds, I went over to Rotterdam to check out security, and once again, the arrangements filled me with trepidation. Feyenoord's officials assured me they were perfectly capable of coping with a European Cup Final, and looking around the stadium, you could see they had much better means of segregation than those we had encountered in Belgium.

But a daunting thought crossed my mind. What use is segregation when there is no proper control over the distribution of tickets? From what I could see, Feyenoord had no qualms about selling blocks of tickets to anyone willing to pay for them. To test my theory, I went up to a ticket kiosk outside the stadium and said I would be bringing over a party of 50 supporters on a coach from England. When I asked if I would be able to buy that number of tickets, I was told "No problem". If I could walk up to a kiosk and buy 50 tickets just like that, so could anyone else, so there was every chance that opposition supporters might end up in the same area of the ground.

Thankfully, it was all right on the night. Although there were a few minor disturbances outside the ground, the problems were nowhere near as bad as Anderlecht. It might well have been different, though, we discovered later, had the police not arrested a number of German supporters for carrying guns.

The Final itself is something of a blur in my mind. I can't say I particularly enjoyed the game. All the organisation involved, and the worry that we might end up with more hooligan problems, had taken the edge off the build-up. In the end, the night just passed me by.

My images of Rotterdam are walking on the pitch with the players before the match, resplendent in my claret blazer and blue shirt; the tumultuous noise from the crowd; the masses of Union Jacks draped in front of our supporters; the delight of Peter Withe's 67th minute goal; the agonising wait for the final whistle.

Even then, it didn't really sink in. There was still work to be done. We had arranged a post-match party at the Apollo Hotel in Amsterdam, and once all the celebrations had died down, the players' wives and girlfriends sped off ahead of us. It was some considerable time later that the players and officials joined them, Ken McNaught being detained for an hour after he was chosen to provide a urine sample.

Once the random drugs test had been completed, we were able to relax, and I'm told it was quite a night in Amsterdam. I can't offer a first hand account because I was absolutely drained by that stage, and headed off to bed early.

The club I had supported since I was old enough to lift my head above the Holte End wall, whom I had followed in an A40 with a temperamental bonnet to places like Rochdale and Halifax, were

Champions of Europe. And all I could think about was getting some sleep!

No doubt the 10,000 fans who went to Rotterdam for the Final will find that hard to believe. Most of them continued their after-match celebrations inside the stadium by partying through the night at bars and clubs. Had I been with them, no doubt I would have done the same. But you have to detach yourself from the euphoria when you are so closely involved with a football club. All the worry, first about the Anderlecht hearing and then about fans' behaviour at the Final, had left me physically and mentally exhausted.

It wasn't until we attended a Civic Reception at Birmingham Council House, and I stood on the balcony gazing at the thousands of people who packed the square outside, that it finally dawned on me what we had achieved, what it meant to the City of Birmingham. As our players might have said, I was over the moon.

Czeching out the European opposition in Geneva.

Chapter Five

Back In The USSR

I thought I'd seen it all during our triumphant European Cup campaign. But the road to Rotterdam – via Iceland, Germany, Russia and Belgium – was just the start of my geography lesson as secretary of a top English football club.

During the course of the following two seasons I sampled the delights of Turkey, Romania, Italy and Portugal, with another trip to the Soviet Union thrown in for good measure. This time, though, it wasn't quite so much of a journey into the unknown. The first leg of our second round UEFA Cup-tie in 1983-84 took us right to the very seat of Communism. And didn't we know it during the build-up to our match against Spartak Moscow!

Our Russian hosts, to be fair, made every effort to make us feel welcome, arranging various excursions for members of the official party. All the same, you were always left with the impression of being shown only what they wanted you to see.

And who knows what might have become of club president Trevor Gill had we not realised he had gone missing after we were taken on a tour of Red Square? Our guided tour of central Moscow could hardly have been more comprehensive, and we were shown many famous landmarks which had previously been just names, including the

Kremlin and Lenin's Tomb. Then we headed back to the hotel, our coach being accompanied by two police bikes at the front and another two at the rear. We must have travelled a mile or so before it suddenly dawned on me that Trevor wasn't with us. I informed the Spartak officials, and without hesitation they went into action. The coach driver made contact with the policemen in front of us, and before I knew it there were sirens wailing and lights flashing as we performed a dramatic U-turn on a busy dual carriageway.

The Spartak people were clearly concerned what might become of Gill if he was left for too long in the middle of Red Square, but thankfully he was standing there, his worried expression turning into a broad smile as he saw us approaching.

During our stay in Moscow, we were also offered the choice of a visit to the Bolshoi Ballet or a tour of the British Embassy. As a lover of the Beatles rather than the ballet, I decided to skip the culture and improve my knowledge of politics. More to the point, it sounded like a good opportunity to phone home. Calls to the UK had proved well nigh impossible from our hotel.

As we were shown around the Embassy, I got chatting to one or two of the staff, and after a while I cheekily asked if I could make a phone call to England. Not a word was offered in response, but I was led into a room and pointed towards a desk with a red telephone. It was only as I started dialling that I looked up to see a notice in large, bold letters: BE CAREFUL, THIS CONVERSATION IS BEING LISTENED TO. I didn't exactly have any Soviet secrets to relay back home, but it was certainly an eerie feeling knowing that every word uttered during that telephone call was being monitored by the KGB.

Perhaps it was that incident which started to make me wary of my counterpart in the Spartak camp. From the moment we had been introduced, he had seemed rather subdued and unwilling to engage in a great deal of idle chat. And although he opened up after a drink or two at the official banquet, he was more miserable than ever the following day. After seeing the warning sign above the Embassy telephone, my imagination started to run wild, and I convinced myself he was a member of the secret police, using his position at the football club as a front.

That conviction started to take deeper root when he made a point of coming to our hotel while we were having lunch with the players on the day of the match, and said he needed to have a word in private with me. My heart was pounding as he led me away to another room. It occurred to me that either I was going to be arrested, or warned about my conduct, even though I couldn't recall doing anything wrong. Or maybe he suspected my bugged telephone call from the Embassy had contained coded messages about life in the Soviet Union.

I still didn't have a clue what was happening when he reached inside his pocket. What was he going to produce? A gun, maybe, or a warrant for my arrest? No, folks, my Russian pal broke into a smile for the first time since we had met – and handed over a tin of caviar. He wanted to give me a present, but obviously could not be seen doing so by the Russian authorities.

Such cautious behaviour should really have been no surprise to me, because I had experienced something similar 12 months earlier when we were in Romania for a European Cup-tie against Dinamo Bucharest. Like the Spartak people, the Dinamo officials also seemed keen to impress us, while keeping their distance.

On the Tuesday morning after our arrival, we were collected by our hosts, who took great pride in showing us around their vast complex. While football was the focal point, it was clear that Dinamo catered for a whole range of other sports, including basketball, hockey and gymnastics. To round off the tour, in fact, we were taken into a huge gymnasium where groups of youngsters were going through their various routines.

The standard of all the kids in that hall was exceptionally high, and we soon discovered why. One of the football club officials called across their coach to say hello to us – and it was none other than Nadia Comaneci, the gymnast whose gold medal achievements and bubbly personality had charmed the world at the 1976 Olympic Games. By the time we met her, she had lost her cheeky, youthful looks and no longer boasted a slender, shapely figure, but you only had to look at the youngsters under her care to see the impact she was making on the future of Romanian gymnastics.

Nadia had a smile for us, too, which was more than could be said for our grim-faced hosts, who gave the impression of looking over their shoulders, and being worried about stepping out of line. They were accompanied constantly by stern-looking gentlemen to whom we were never introduced, and I suspect these silent shadows were security officers. Even when we were taken into the Dinamo committee room, and offered glasses of vodka which we were expected to knock back in one gulp, the faces of the Dinamo officials and their mysterious friends never cracked. It didn't help, either, that none of them seemed to speak English, and we certainly couldn't converse in their language.

Dinamo's directors still had the look of men about to be sent to Siberia when they arrived at our hotel at lunchtime on the day of the match, but we noticed one subtle difference. There was no sign of their dark-suited associates. After everyone had piled into a limousine, we headed for the centre of Bucharest, and I couldn't help noticing that as we got closer and closer, and the streets became busy with traffic, the limo actually gathered speed. It was a pretty hair-raising experience, particularly when I looked out and saw people leaping out of our way. Wherever we were going, the Dinamo people certainly wanted to get there in a hurry, and without being followed.

Suddenly, without warning, the vehicle screeched to a halt, and we were ushered on to the pavement and into a large hall with military precision. Once inside, the doors slammed behind us, and as everyone filed upstairs, I could hear the limousine roar away, no doubt to give a few more locals the fright of their lives.

What the chauffeur was actually doing, we quickly discovered, was making sure any pursuing secret agents would be directed well away from where the gathering of Dinamo Bucharest and Aston Villa directors was taking place. There was nothing particularly sinister about this James Bond-style operation, the Dinamo officials simply wanted to have a good time without appearing to be fraternising with capitalists from the West.

You wouldn't believe the change in attitude once we were safely ensconced in that upstairs room, away from the watchful eye of Romanian government officers. It was almost as if our hosts had undergone a personality implant. What's more, it turned out they could speak English after all, and once the formalities of the occasion had been dispensed with we had a wonderful time.

For three hours or more, we ate, we drank, we exchanged stories, we sang songs. Once they knew they weren't being watched, these guys certainly knew how to let their hair down. At one stage, after a few straight vodkas had been consumed, they were even dancing on the tables. By the time the party broke up, everyone was on first name terms, and there was a great deal of hand-shaking and embracing before the limousine returned to take us back to our hotel.

Two hours before kick-off they arrived, as arranged, to take us the unusually-named Stadionul 23 August, which is, apparently, a reference to the date of the first uprising against the occupying Germans in 1944. Although I had showered and changed, I was still glowing from the earlier festivities, and I greeted one of the Dinamo directors with a huge grin and a few words of English. This was a mistake. He curtly shook my hand, and his grim-faced expression gave every indication that not only did he not understand me, but that we had never met before.

As I glanced behind him, I could see the reason for the cool reception from someone who had earlier hugged me like a lifelong pal. The security men were back on the scene, and looking sterner than ever. No doubt they were more than a little displeased about being given the slip that afternoon.

We sat side by side with our drinking pals throughout the match, but there was no joviality on this occasion. They had been clearly ordered not to socialise with us, and although 70,000 Romanians created an amazing atmosphere inside the stadium, we just sat there stone-faced. Even when Gary Shaw scored the goals which gave us a 2-0 first leg lead, myself and everyone else in the Villa party had to resist the temptation to show any emotion. Needless to say, we made amends on the plane back to Birmingham!

Chapter Six

The Two Ronnies

The only thing they had in common was their Christian name, but few people have made such an impact on Aston Villa as Ron Saunders and Ron Atkinson. They are, without question, the two most single-minded men ever to manage the club, even if their approach to the job was totally different. Which just goes to prove there are no set rules when it comes to being successful in football.

Saunders was deadly serious in everything he did, a deep thinking-man who rarely showed any sign of humour and frequently put the fear of God into the players in his charge. Atkinson was flamboyant, charismatic and quick-witted, never happier than when he was holding court with players, coaches and anyone else willing to gather around him and listen to his tales.

Between them, they were in control of Villa's destiny on the pitch for 11 years, and they left a lasting impression on everyone who came into contact with them, albeit for vastly contrasting reasons.

Ron Saunders was a real Sergeant Major character, a strict disciplinarian who insisted on things being done his way, although I can't deny I have a lot to thank him for. When Alan Bennett announced he was leaving Villa to become secretary of Leicester City in March 1979, the club had to find a successor, and although I was 28, and had been assistant to Alan for more than six years, I was reluctant to apply for the job.

But after chairman Harry Kartz interviewed several other candidates, Saunders kept asking me why I didn't go for it. My answer was that I didn't feel I was ready for such an important role, but he not only convinced me I would be able to cope, but offered to help me out whenever I was uncertain about anything.

Obviously I was very grateful for Ron's support and encouragement. I wasn't what you would describe as an outgoing sort of person, and I approached my new position with a certain amount of apprehension. But a few days after my appointment Ron called all the players together and told them: "This is Aston Villa's new secretary. From now on you don't call him Steve, you address him as Mr Stride." He also insisted that they showed me respect, and to be fair the players did, which boosted my confidence enormously.

The problem, though, was that I always felt I was working for Ron Saunders, rather than for the football club. He had coaxed me into applying for the job, and it put me in a position where I felt beholden to him. Some of the young players who came up through our youth and reserve teams must have known the same feeling when Ron gave them their first team chance. If he spotted weakness or uncertainty in anyone, he would pick on them mercilessly, as people like Gary Shaw and Tony Morley will tell you. Those two always seemed to be on the receiving end of tongue-lashings from the manager, while senior professionals such as Peter Withe and Dennis Mortimer escaped lightly because they could stand up to him.

It wasn't only the younger players who came in for the heavy-handed Saunders treatment, though. He had little respect for Doug Ellis, either, and, unfortunately, was not afraid to let it be known. Once, when I was still assistant secretary, the team coach was due to leave Villa Park at 10.30am for an away match at Manchester City. At 10.31, the chairman had not arrived, so Ron told the driver: "Right, we're off."

When Doug turned up a few minutes later, he was understandably furious that the team had gone without him. We jumped in his car and raced up the M6 until we caught up with the coach, flagging the driver down so Doug could complete his journey with the players. I then returned to Villa Park in Doug's car, so I wasn't privy to the conversation between chairman and manager before they reached Maine Road, but I imagine the atmosphere was pretty frosty!

Saunders was equally rigid about adhering to arrangements on trips abroad. He didn't mind the players having a drink in the hotel bar after a day's training, but would always summon his backroom people and anyone else in the travelling party to his room.

We would sit there while Saunders, who was heavily into self-analysis, offered all manner of theories on the meaning of life. These sessions, sometimes lasting for hours, were the last thing we wanted when we could have been downstairs enjoying a drink. But everyone – Ron's assistant Roy McLaren, physio Jim Williams, myself, club doctor David Targett, and even the tour organisers – felt obliged to attend.

After a number of trips, "Doc" Targett and I came to realise the only way to get out of the room when the manager was in full flow was to feign tiredness and say we were off to bed. Doc and I worked out a code, whereby one of us would start yawning and both of us would then make our excuses before retiring, not to our bedrooms, but down to the bar. Sometimes even this ploy didn't work, with Ron so insistent on completing his story that we simply couldn't get away.

When he snapped : "Sit down, you can't be tired yet", we didn't dare argue, dutifully listening and nodding in agreement until Ron had finished. On one occasion, however, Doc and I did manage to make an early escape. We were on a pre-season visit to Germany in the summer of 1980, not long after Peter Withe had joined Villa from Newcastle United for what was then a club record £500,000. As usual, we were ensconced in Ron's room at the Gut Hoene hotel in Dusseldorf, but Doc and I were determined to make a quick exit.

After maybe half an hour or so, I went through the usual yawning routine, explaining that I needed an early night. Amazingly, there was no protest from Ron, and when Doc joined me in the corridor 10 minutes later, we could barely believe our luck. Like a couple of schoolboys playing truant, we rushed downstairs to the bar, where the players were highly amused by the story of our getaway.

They were even more amused a little while later when, under the influence of a Bacardi and Coke or two, everyone began singing raucous songs, and Doc and I found ourselves the centre of attention as we started dancing on the tables. Our performance was going down brilliantly with players and locals alike, until Doc suddenly came to a halt, his face turning a ghostly shade of white. I thought he had been taken ill, until I glanced across to the far side of the room and saw the reason for his discomfort. Ron Saunders was standing there, watching our impromptu dance routine.

Just imagine the embarrassment of two supposedly mature and responsible members of the tour party. Not only had we been caught slipping away for a drink when we had said we were off to bed, but we were making total fools of ourselves in front of arguably the strictest manager in Villa's history. To be fair, Ron never said a word. He just gave us a wry smile which suggested he would find a way of taking his revenge for being duped.

That wasn't the only time I suffered a feeling of acute awkwardness at the hands of RS. During a trip to Majorca, we were staying at the Son Vida hotel in Palma, and at around 3 o'clock one morning I was awakened by a knock at my bedroom door. Half asleep, I stumbled across the room to open it – and immediately realised I had made a mistake. In walked two of the club's biggest practical jokers, Ken McNaught and Jimmy Rimmer, the goalkeeper whose favourite trick was to drop his false teeth in your drink while you weren't looking.

I would happily have settled for the false teeth treatment that night, but Messrs Rimmer and McNaught had something more devious in mind. They picked up my telephone, dialled Ron's room number and yelled a few choice phrases at the boss before slamming down the receiver. Thankfully, they left the room soon afterwards, but if I thought that was the end of the matter, I was mistaken. The next morning at breakfast, Ron said he wanted everyone in our party to gather around the hotel swimming pool for an important meeting.

Once we had all assembled, he informed us: "Last night I received an obscene telephone call in my room. I have checked with the hotel switchboard, and they have traced the room from which the call was made, so I am aware who did it. I'll be dealing with the matter in due course."

I stood there rooted to the spot, and although I hadn't done anything, I felt my face go bright red. Ron was bluffing, but I wasn't to know that at the time. I spent the rest of the trip feeling uneasy to say the least, convinced that Saunders thought I was the culprit. I did learn an important lesson, however. If ever you're abroad with a football team and there's a knock on your door in the middle of the night, ignore it!

To people outside Aston Villa, Saunders' departure from the club in February 1982 must have come as an enormous shock. This was the man who had led the club to promotion from the old Second Division, two League Cup successes, and English football's greatest accolade, the First Division Championship. He had also steered Villa to the quarter-finals of the European Cup, and is undoubtedly the most successful manager in the club's history.

For the best part of eight years he had ruled the team with an iron fist, and his no-nonsense policy had yielded rich dividends. Yet anyone closely connected with Villa at the time he left will tell you they were not altogether surprised. Ron's downfall was that he was unwilling to restrict his authority to the confines of the playing staff. He wanted to be involved in all aspects of running the club, and you won't find a chairman anywhere in football who is willing to tolerate that.

Chairman Ron Bendall certainly wasn't happy about Saunders' increasing interference in affairs beyond his managerial brief, and let it be known. Not surprisingly, this created an uneasy distance between the two men, and the atmosphere could be pretty frosty whenever they were in contact with each other. The situation came to a head one day when Saunders asked a member of the office staff to do something for him. When the chairman heard about it, he was furious, ordering that Saunders' instruction should be ignored. It was as if the two men were testing each other's influence within the club, and Saunders should really have known better than to think he could win such a power struggle. No matter how successful a manager may be, he is ultimately answerable to his chairman, and it was a lesson Saunders failed to heed.

Not long afterwards, he handed in his notice, claiming he was leaving because his authority had been undermined. But right to the end he retained the ability to make me feel ill at ease. I was the first person at the club to become aware of his resignation, Ron phoning me at home to inform me of his decision.

"I've had enough," he told me in his usual matter-of-fact manner. "I'm giving in my notice, would you mind coming round to pick it up?" Even though he was about to leave, and I would no longer have to feel indebted to him, it still seemed more like an order than a request, so I dutifully drove to Ron's house to collect his letter of resignation.

Not content with getting me to act as his messenger, he then asked me to ring the chairman, so he could hear Bendall's reaction. It was a call I would have preferred to make in the privacy of my own home, but Ron insisted. If he was looking for the satisfaction of shocking the chairman, however, he must have been bitterly disappointed.

When I informed Bendall what was happening, the response was calm and composed. "That's okay," he said."If the man wants to leave, I'm not going to beg him to stay. We'll sort things out and move on from here."

Ron subsequently became manager of Birmingham City, while the team he had built went on to win the European Cup. He will always be remembered as the man who guided Villa to the League title for the first time in 71 years, and if pride hadn't got in the way, he would have also experienced the glory of Rotterdam. Who knows what he might have gone on to achieve from there?

As it was, he never scaled such great heights again, finishing his career with West Bromwich Albion after his spell at St Andrew's – and we had to wait more than a decade before the club's next major trophy came along. That was masterminded by the other Ron – Atkinson – who enjoyed a considerably shorter reign in the Villa hot seat, but nevertheless made an equally stunning impact.

The team's playing record was nowhere near as impressive under Atkinson as it had been in the Saunders era, but there is no question that during the three years and four months Big Ron was in charge, Villa received more media exposure than ever before. Graham Taylor had begun the task of reviving the "sleeping giant" by leading us back to the top flight and into Europe, and while the season under Jo Venglos had been something of a siesta, the club awoke with a vengeance when Ron sent his champagne image gushing through the corridors of Villa Park.

Big, bold and forceful, he arrived in July 1991 with a promise to shake things up after the previous season's flirtation with relegation, and was as good as his word. While the addition to our honours list was restricted to a single Coca-Cola Cup triumph, there was never a dull moment while Ron was at the helm. He raised Villa's profile to unprecedented heights, and his sheer reputation was instrumental in persuading a succession of big-name players to join us, people like Steve Staunton, Dalian Atkinson, Dean Saunders, Ray Houghton, Earl Barrett and Andy Townsend. And it wasn't just when dealing with footballers that he employed his immense powers of persuasion.

I was treated to a classic example of Ron's sheer bravado when I accompanied him to the 1992 European Championship Final in Sweden. This may sound a straightforward exercise for the manager and secretary of one of England's top clubs, but there was a slight problem to be overcome. I didn't have a ticket, and Germany v Denmark in Gothenburg was one of those occasions where no amount of contacts within the game was likely to produce one, particularly as I decided to attend the match only a few days before it took place.

I should explain that originally I had no intention of going to any of the the matches in Sweden. But when war-torn Yugoslavia withdrew just before the tournament started and were replaced by Denmark, my interest began to mount. The Danish squad included Kent Nielsen, who had become a good friend during his time with Villa, and had left us earlier that year to join Aarhus in his home country. Basically, he wasn't Ron's type of player, but my opinion, for what it's worth, is that Kent still had a lot of football left in him.

So he proved on his return to Denmark, and having re-established himself as a regular member of the Danish team, he now found himself plunged, along with his team-mates, into the Finals of a championship which is second only to the World Cup. Denmark, to be fair, were regarded as little more than makeweights at Euro 92. While the other seven finalists had been preparing for months, the Danes had barely a couple of weeks to get themselves ready for the big event after being informed by UEFA that they would take Yugoslavia's place in the Finals. They were also in the same group as England, France and host nation Sweden, and popular opinion was that you could perm any two from those three to qualify for the semi-finals.

It was little more than a tongue in cheek remark, then, when I told Kent during a telephone conversation just before the championships: "If you get to the Final, I'll be there." A few weeks later, after Denmark had not only qualified from their group, but had beaten Holland in a penalty shoot-out in the semi-final, it was time to make good my promise.

First, the easy part. Ron was covering the match as a commentator for ITV, and we flew out to Gothenburg together on the day before the Final. He also managed to get me a room at the hotel where he was staying, despite the fact that most beds in the city had been pre-booked months in advance. All the same, the fact that I didn't have a ticket was still nagging away at the back of my mind, but every time I broached the subject, Ron merely shrugged his shoulders and said: "Don't worry, pal." On the day of the game, Ron, Republic of Ireland manager Jack Charlton and myself were driven to the Ullevi Stadium by former Millwall goalkeeper Brian King, who was now working in Sweden and acting as a link man for ITV.

Ron and Jack seemed quite amused by my concern over my lack of a ticket, but I was beginning to get more and more worried in case I ended up being left outside the ground. I wasn't totally convinced, either, when Jack took his identity tag, complete with photograph, from around his neck and handed it to me. "Put that on and you won't have a problem," he told me. "But make sure you wear it with the reverse showing – you don't look anything like me!"

I felt as guilty as hell as we approached the security man at the media entrance, but thankfully he must have associated my red face with the fact that it was a hot day. We sailed through with no difficulty, and I watched the Euro 92 Final from the television gantry. It was a great occasion, too, and I took real delight from seeing Kent help Denmark to a shock 2-0 win over Germany, who had been favourites right from the start of the tournament. Big Ron may not have rated Kent as a player, but he made sure I was there to witness my Nordic friend's finest hour.

I always enjoyed Ron's company on trips abroad. He's the sort of charismatic guy who loves having people around him, either as an audience for his endless stream of witty one-liners, or to test their sporting knowledge. Whenever he had a group of football people around him, he loved to get everyone involved by throwing out questions which got everyone involved in an informal quiz situation.

This frequently involved lists of achievements, and on one trip to Germany he once announced: "Right, let's name all the FA Cup winners since the War." One by one, we went through the years, sometimes naming the winners straight away, sometimes hesitating before someone came up with the correct team. But I reckon the joke was on Ron when we reached 1983 – everyone's faces went blank, and one or two of the party started scratching their heads in mock concentration. We all knew, of course, that Manchester United had won the Cup that year, and that Atkinson had been their manager. Initially, he looked dumbfounded that no-one could produce the answer, but suddenly it dawned on him we were winding him up, and a characteristic cheeky grin spread across his face.

Once we had brought the FA Cup up to date (including a little more manufactured hesitation over 1985, the second time United won it under Ron's management), we moved on to League Cup winners since the competition's inception in 1960-61. And so it went on as we tried to recall Grand National winners, Derby winners, Wimbledon champions, Open golf champions, County cricket champions. When it seemed we had exhausted every sporting subject, Ron had everyone rolling with laughter as he suddenly announced: "Here's one for you. Name all the Boat Race winners since the War!"

That was typical of the man's quick wit, and he was never happier than when he was taking centre stage among people within the game. During his time with Villa, that usually meant spending most of his time with his backroom staff and players at our Bodymoor Heath training ground. We hardly ever saw him at Villa Park. Ron has never been an office-based person, and he made it clear from day one that he regarded Bodymoor as his place of work.

On the face of it, there's no problem with the tracksuit approach. A manager is judged by what he achieves with his players, so you can hardly criticise anyone for spending so much time with the team. But there is still a considerable amount of administration on which a manager needs to be consulted, and his reluctance to come to Villa Park on anything other than match days made my life difficult to say the least.

Three or four times a day, Ron would ring me from the mobile phone in his car, usually on his way to or from training, and the line was invariably crackly and unclear, so we frequently ended up shouting to make each other heard. At times it became embarrassing as I was forced to yell details of confidential club business, sometimes including details of players' contracts down the phone. It reached the stage where I almost dreaded the ring of that telephone, followed by Ron's customary "Hiya, pal."

If Atkinson was reluctant to come to the ground in person, he was never backwards in coming forwards when it came to asking for Directors' Box tickets. Often, too, he would leave it until the last minute before informing me he required extra tickets, which usually meant the whole seating plan had to be reorganised.

For away matches, we receive 20 Directors' Box passes, and these are normally distributed among our own board members and guests well before the game. When the team arrived at around 2pm, though, you could bet Ron would seek me out with a request for additional tickets for his friends, which meant I had to pull a few strings with my counterpart at the home club to accommodate him.

I once took the precaution of warning him two weeks in advance that I was struggling for passes for a match at Arsenal because of the demands of our directors. This turned out to be a mistake. Ignoring my predicament, Ron stated in a matter-of-fact manner that he needed four tickets, and once again I had to go through the business of making sure they were left for collection.

Imagine my annoyance, then, when I looked around just after the kick-off at Highbury to discover why Ron's need had been so pressing. Two of the seats he had demanded were occupied by players who were not in the side that day, and the other two were empty. So much for the manager needing four passes. He had said it merely to make the point that he felt he was entitled to them.

If my early warning system backfired badly on that occasion, I was guilty of another mistake concerning Ron before a game at Villa Park. His policy was to watch the first half from the Directors' Box, and he always sat next to me, chuntering away about what was happening out on the pitch. Usually, I didn't take a great deal of notice of what he was saying, but on this particular occasion, he suddenly asked: "Hey pal, who's that sitting next to the chairman?" My initial reaction was to give him a clever retort, like: "Don't you recognise the England manager?" but before the words left my lips, I sensibly thought better of it.

Ron didn't need telling that it was Terry Venables who was chatting to Doug Ellis. He was letting me know that as club secretary, I should have informed him that the England coach would be attending the game. He was absolutely right, too. I had overlooked one of my duties, and it bothered me for the rest of the day. Knowing Ron, he probably forgot all about my oversight straight away, and he certainly never mentioned it again.

There was never a dull moment when Ron was around, and the club enjoyed a sizable helping of success under his guidance, including a memorable 1994 Coca-Cola Cup Final triumph over Manchester United. It was Villa's first major honour for 12 years, and at Wembley that March evening, you would have bet your mortgage on Big Fat Ron's claret-and-blue army going from strength to strength.

While Wembley glory gave us all a tremendous shot in the arm, though, the team's League form had been causing concern in the build-up to the Final, and continued to do so for the remainder of that season and into the next. By the time our lads chucked away a 3-1 lead to lose 4-3 to Wimbledon on a cold November night at Selhurst Park, they had mustered just four wins in 23 Premiership matches, and there was talk of relegation in the air.

The long journey back from South London, never a bundle of laughs at the best of times, seemed endless that Wednesday night. I drove, Doug Ellis talked. And it was clear he had more on his mind than just another defeat. The chairman was deeply concerned that poor results had almost become the norm since Wembley, and he could sense that supporters, previously 100 per cent behind Atkinson, were beginning to turn against the manager.

By the early hours of the following morning, as we finally arrived back in Birmingham after a long, tiring journey, Doug had made up his mind: Ron had to go. While the team were unquestionably playing better than their results indicated, the chairman bravely took the decision that a change of manager was required.

A secret Board meeting was held over lunch at the New Hall Hotel in Sutton Coldfield, and after the decision had been formally approved by the other directors, we adjourned to Villa Park for another meeting, which Ron was asked to attend.

I'm convinced it came as a bolt out of the blue to the manager when, after exchanging a few niceties, he was told: "Sorry, Ron we're dispensing with your services." Earlier in the day, apparently, he had told Midland media men he might have to sign a prolific goalscorer like Stan Collymore to get Villa away from the relegation zone, and I'm sure he turned up at the Board meeting expecting to be asked which players he wanted to buy.

One look at his face was all I needed to see how genuinely shocked he was, but he quickly regained his composure, and calmly discussed the termination of his contract before leaving the room. I don't think a managerial sacking at Aston Villa has ever sparked quite so much controversy. Two weeks elapsed before Brian Little was appointed as Atkinson's successor, and throughout that period the local papers and radio stations were inundated with letters and calls from supporters, some claiming the club had made an almighty blunder, others that a parting of the ways was inevitable.

As for Ron, he took it all in his stride after the initial shock. When he faced the cameras for a television interview about his sacking, he was as bubbly and quick-witted as ever, signing off with the classic line: "I was going to buy Collymore, now I'm going to buy Cauliflower!"

Chapter Seven

Czech Mate

Whatever is best for Aston Villa, you must do. Don't worry about me, I will be okay. You must do what is right for the club. That's the most important thing."

Those words, believe it or not, were uttered by a man on the brink of losing his job after less than 12 months at the helm. I'm sure any English manager would have been rather less understanding, but Dr Jozef Venglos was different to anyone, manager or otherwise, I have come across in football. He was the perfect gentleman, never anything less than courteous, and he certainly showed me more respect than any other Villa manager – even if I could never quite come to terms with him addressing me as Mr Secretary General!

Dr Jo was appointed in the summer of 1990, after Graham Taylor had left to become England manager, after we had been linked with all manner of other names, from Franz Beckenbauer to Joe Jordan. By comparison, Venglos was very much an unknown quantity, although he had just guided Czechoslovakia to the quarter-finals of the World Cup in Italy, and was a highly respected coach on the Continent.

Unfortunately, the game in this country is far different to anything he had ever come across, and Jo, despite his astute tactical mind, never got to grips with handling English footballers. As a disciplined man, he expected his players to display similar qualities, but the mentality of players over here was different to anything he had experienced.

No-one likes losing football matches, but Jo took every defeat to heart, even apologising to me for the team's performance every time we lost. That was something I had never encountered before, and I must admit it became a little embarrassing after a while. Jo could never quite comprehend, either, how our players could enjoy a beer and socialise with their friends and family barely half an hour after they had lost a game. He couldn't grasp that in their minds, the game was over, they had done their best, and there was little point in dwelling on the outcome. Jo always felt there should be a funeral atmosphere in the players' lounge or on the team coach after a defeat.

His wife Eva also felt the pressure. Towards the end of the season, after the team had left the field to booing after their latest reversal, she was chatting to a few of the other wives.

Eva's command of English was not as good as Jo's, and when she muttered "Poor my husband", one of the other ladies came to her assistance, saying: "You mean, my poor husband." To which Eva replied: "Yes, him too!"

He was never really tuned in to the thinking of his backroom staff, either. Like the players, our assistant manager John Ward and coach Dennis Booth also enjoyed a laugh and a joke after a game. Their attitude was to try and forget what couldn't be changed, and look forward positively to the next match, whereas Jo was usually pre-occupied in analysing every move, and trying to work out what had gone wrong. Such an attitude is commendable, of course, but it meant he was never able to establish a rapport with his staff and his team.

Mid-way through that season, an attempt was made to switch to Jo's way of thinking, which resulted in the dismissal of Ward and the appointment of Peter Withe, the club's 1982 European Cup hero, as assistant manager. But even that did not prevent our slide down the table, and when we only narrowly escaped relegation, a parting of the ways became inevitable.

For all that, however, Venglos endeared himself to a lot of people at Villa Park with his modest courtesy, and everyone at the club was angry when the Birmingham Evening Mail ran a back page headline in large red type: *For God's Sake GO Dr Jo!* We had lost 5-1 at home to Manchester City the previous night, and our situation looked pretty grim, but everyone at the club was appalled at such a hatchet job by the local evening paper, and I wrote to the Mail telling them so.

Thankfully, we managed to avoid the drop, but I believe any hope of genuine understanding between Jo and the players disappeared in the course of a couple of incidents during our end-of-season trip to Malaysia. It was a very informal trip, intended as a wind-down after a hard, gruelling campaign, although it didn't quite turn out that way. To be honest, it was a catalogue of disasters. For starters, we had to travel via Copenhagen, and we had a five-hour wait in Denmark, which didn't exactly get the tour off to a flying start.

Then we had to stop in Singapore for refuelling, and we had to sit in a hot aircraft on the runway for three hours for no apparent reason before the captain was given the go-ahead to take off. There was great relief all round when the plane started moving, but no sooner had our hopes of completing the journey been raised, than we ground to a halt again. This time we were at least informed what the problem was. There had been a fire on a plane at Sarawak airport, the runway was blocked, and we would have to spend the night in Singapore.

Eventually we reached our destination the following day, but by then most of the players would happily have flown straight home. Trips to such exotic places may seem appealing, but footballers have to do so much travelling during the course of a season that they are often less than enthusiastic about end-of-season tours and extra matches. The rigours of a long, hard season had obviously begun to tell on the manager, too, as I discovered when I was in the dressing room before one of our friendlies out there.

An hour or so before kick-off, Jo announced the team, and something didn't quite ring true as he named a goalkeeper, four defenders and five midfielders. Everyone in the room was convinced he had decided to play with just one up front, but Jo rounded off his proposed line-up with two strikers. I can't remember who it was, but one of the lads plucked up the courage to say: "Boss, that's 12 players!" Ian Ormondroyd, our 6ft 5in striker, immediately volunteered to stand down, and I got the impression the rest of the players would just as happily have dropped out, rather than playing a meaningless friendly in a sweltering, humid atmosphere.

It was on the same trip that Paul McGrath and Tony Cascarino were required to fly home early to join up with the international squad, which effectively meant they had to miss our second game. Jo, however, was conscious of being seen to do the right thing, and did not want to disappoint our Malaysian hosts by leaving out two of our star men.

The compromise was that McGrath and Cascarino would start the game, but would then be substituted at half-time so they could rush to the airport to catch their flight home. Jo took it upon himself to book a taxi, giving the driver instructions where to be and at what time. Just imagine the scene, then, as the second half kicked off with our manager pacing up and down the touchline, gazing into the stand instead of at the pitch. As the minutes ticked by, he became more and more agitated, continually consulting his watch, until a relieved look spread across his face. The taxi driver had arrived.

Substitutions are usually made because of injury or lack or form, but I never thought I would see the day when two players were replaced at half-time because they had a taxi waiting for them. It was that sort of match, though, and later I witnessed something else I'd never seen before – a linesman flagging for offside against one of our substitutes, a young lad called Darrell Duffy, who was warming up on the touchline.

Not long afterwards, Jo left the club by mutual consent, but if he never truly commanded the respect of our players, it was certainly a different story in his home country. I discovered that when chairman

Doug Ellis and I accompanied him to Czechoslovakia to sign Ivo Stas from Banik Ostrava. On our second night in Prague, when the endless transfer forms had been completed, Jo recommended a plush restaurant for dinner, and we took a cab from our hotel to the city centre. As soon as we stepped on to the pavement, there were calls of "Good evening, Dr Venglos" from passers-by who regarded Jo as a national hero for guiding the Czech team to the quarter-finals of *Italia 90* earlier that year.

The restaurant we visited clearly had a good reputation. They were turning people away as we arrived, and having made no reservation, I fully expected that we would also have to look elsewhere for something to eat. Once the proprietor spotted Dr Jo, however, we were immediately shown to the best table (I somehow had a vision of three people being shot so we could be accommodated), and proceeded to enjoy a magnificent four-course dinner which would not have been out of place in the West End. With wine and drinks on top, I estimated the cost would be around £90, even allowing for the fact that this was Eastern Europe and not central London.

After several minutes studying the bill, however, I concluded that the total charge for our gourmet evening at one of Prague's most fashionable establishments was just over £12. Either my conversion calculations had been clouded by the local lager, or we had been seriously undercharged. Not wishing to take advantage of the situation, I whispered to Jo that it looked as if a mistake had been made.

As always when confronted by a problem, Jo looked deeply hurt and offended. "Do you think it is too expensive?" he asked, and before I had time to point out that we would have paid almost as much for fish and chips three times in Perry Barr, he added: "If you are not happy, I will question it with them."

As we walked out of that restaurant, I half expected to be pursued by waiters demanding that we settle the rest of the bill, but there was no such problem. Czech prices are cheap, I know, but I reckon Jo must have pulled a few strings with the management that night.

At least I was able to return the favour by inviting him to my home for a meal, although even then he arrived laden with a bottle of vodka and various other gifts. That was typical of Jo's generous nature, and while he may be regarded as a failure in terms of managing Aston Villa, I will always have the greatest respect for him.

It was certainly a pleasure to meet him again when he came to Villa Park with the Czech Republic for the 1996 European Championship Finals. Five years had passed since I had seen him, but little had changed, really. He was involved with the national team once again – and still referred to me as Mr Secretary General. I was just grateful he no longer had to apologise for poor results.

Chapter Eight

Meals On Wheels

When Brian Little joined us from Leicester City in November, 1994, he became the ninth manager to take charge of Villa's playing fortunes during my time with the club. In one way or another, those nine lives have all had an effect on my own, because I have inevitably had to organise the administration behind any decisions they have made. Whether they have been buying, selling or offering new contracts, I've had to get involved in the paperwork at some stage.

My relationships with our managers have been varied. Some have become good friends, others I've hardly known beyond the day-to-day routine of club business.

Vic Crowe, for instance, rarely crossed my path. Although I had stood in his sweet shop during his playing days, in the hope of seeing him behind the counter, I never had a great deal to do with him once I was on the staff. I was only Alan Bennett's assistant at that time, so my contact with the manager was very limited. Vic, who was in charge when I joined the club, came across as a fairly quiet sort of person, although his Welsh background did, occasionally, result in the odd outburst of temper.

That was certainly never true of Tony Barton, a lovely guy whose level-headed approach was a crucial factor in our European Cup triumph. A lot of managers would have been eager to stamp their own authority on the job after taking over from Ron Saunders, but Tony was sensible enough to appreciate the quality of the team he inherited when he stepped up from the position of assistant manager.

We were through to the European quarter-finals by the time Tony moved into the hot seat, and he believed the team were good enough to go on and win the competition. That was why he let things run their course, rather than trying to impose himself on the job. There was, however, one crucial difference. Under the previous manager, the players had always felt they were ruled with an iron fist. Tony's more laid-back approach went a long way to relaxing them in readiness for our last three European ties, against Dynamo Kiev, Anderlecht and Bayern Munich.

In the long-term, unfortunately, Tony's mild manner probably cost him his job. Although we fared pretty well over the next couple of seasons, he never seemed completely at ease about being at the helm. Although he coped well under the unwelcome glare of the spotlight, I always got the impression he would have been much happier continuing as a right-hand man rather than a manager.

While you couldn't help but like Tony Barton, it was with his successor, Graham Turner, that I forged the strongest of my friendships with any of the Villa managers I've known. No doubt the public's view of Graham was that he was a serious, solemn man. He rarely smiled during matches, and frequently had the look of someone with all the cares of the world on his shoulders.

Away from the pressures of the job, though, you couldn't wish to meet a more friendly, easy-going guy. My wife Carolyn and I became good friends with Graham and his wife Ann during his time as manager, and we still see each other on occasions. It's the sort of relationship where we may not have any contact for months at a time, but when we get together, it's almost as if we had seen each other only a week earlier.

The four of us used to belong to what we called *The Dinner Club*, which also included Villa's director and medical officer David Targett, Birmingham restaurant owner Eric Chan and former Holiday Inn banqueting manager Erol Olcan, and their wives.

Our party of 10 dined out regularly in the Birmingham area, and we had some great times because we all had a similar sense of humour. I vividly recall one meal at Birmingham's Midland Hotel. We had arranged to meet at 7.30pm, but half an hour later, "Doc" Targett and his wife Anne had not arrived. Doc eventually turned up, explaining that Anne had been taken ill. We told him to just enjoy a starter and then go home to her, but once he'd relaxed over a glass of wine and started chatting away, he seemed to forget all about her. He eventually got home at 2 o'clock the following morning!

Another of our *Dinner Club* evenings ended on a rather less pleasant note. It was a Friday night at the end of the 1985-86 season, just after we had finished a disappointing 16th in the table. Even though the season was over, Graham was driving to Glasgow the following day to watch the Scottish Cup Final and run the rule over potential new signings for the following season, so he didn't want a late night.

Throughout our meal I had the uncomfortable feeling that another diner was watching us – and not looking at all happy that we were having an enjoyable time. My suspicions were confirmed as we left the restaurant.

The fellow, obviously a Villa supporter, shouted across to Graham: "How can you enjoy yourself after the crap season we have just had?"

Although I'm an easy-going sort of person, it made my blood boil to see our manager having to put up with such verbal abuse during a night out with friends, particularly as it was the end of the season. Graham, to his credit, displayed great restraint, refusing to respond to this loud-mouth's insults, but the incident put a damper on what had been a great meal at Eric Chan's new restaurant.

Graham brought in three new players that summer, Aberdeen

midfielder Neale Cooper, Sheffield Wednesday's Birmingham-born striker Garry Thompson and Andy Gray, who rejoined the club after spells with Wolves and Everton. The fees amounted to around £1m, which was a substantial outlay at the time, but it proved to be a classic case of money failing to buy success. You might say, in fact, that in this instance, money bought failure. We were relegated the following season.

By then, Graham had been ousted from the managerial hot seat. A 6-0 drubbing at Nottingham Forest proved to be the final nail in his coffin, that setback leaving us with just one win and five defeats from the opening half dozen matches.

Just as new players can't just wave a magic wand, however, neither can new managers. Graham's replacement, Billy McNeill, was already having a rough time at Manchester City when he joined us, and he ended up with the unwanted distinction of being the manager of two clubs who were relegated in the same season.

From the time of his arrival in September, to his departure by mutual consent the following May, I never felt McNeill's heart was in the job. The former Scottish international never made any attempt to move to the Midlands, and there were constant rumours that he was merely marking time before taking over at Celtic, the club he had graced as a player.

McNeill was not only the shortest-serving manager I have known during my time at Villa, he was also the least amenable. He always kept himself at a distance, and it was no surprise to any of us when he headed back north of the border to become Celtic's manager within days of leaving us.

He did, at least, earn himself a nickname among the players. During team-talks apparently, he would talk them through tactical moves which invariably ended with the phrase "...and bingo!", suggesting that a goal was bound to result from the build-up he had just described. This amused the players, even though he was deadly serious. Before long, he became known as *Billy McBingo*.

McNeill's departure left us looking for our third manager in less than 12 months. We had undeniably slipped up with his appointment, but there's no doubt that we got it right next time.

Graham Taylor effectively had a job for life at Watford, having guided the Vicarage Road club from the old Fourth Division to the top flight, as well as taking them to the FA Cup Final. Even so, he found the challenge of taking over a famous club like Villa irresistible, despite the fact we had just gone down.

Because Graham's name was synonymous with Watford, I don't think we would even have made an approach had it not been for a tip-off from one of the club's former managers. Dick Taylor, who had been in charge of Villa's playing fortunes during the mid-1960s, was now running a sports shop, and knew Graham and his family well.

It was through Dick that chairman Doug Ellis became aware that, despite his affinity to the Hornets, and his close friendship with Watford's megastar owner Elton John, Graham might just be tempted to follow the Yellow Brick Road to Villa Park.

When Graham was invited to come and talk things over with us, it wasn't so much an interview, more a case of discussing his contract details. He knew, and we knew, that the job was his if he wanted it.

Once installed, Graham made it clear that the laid-back regime which had been the trademark of McNeill's reign was a thing of the past. He described the set-up at our Bodymoor Heath training ground as "a shambles", and quickly set about imposing some discipline on the players.

Graham was a stickler for doing things properly. During his first season, he even insisted on the players spending the night before home matches in a local hotel, although it is one of our overnight stays in another part of the country which provides one of my most enduring memories of the man who was later to become England manager.

We had an important match at Reading the following day, but once the players had gone to bed, the rest of us gathered in the hotel bar for a "nightcap". When football managers and coaches are in full flow, sessions like this can go on for quite some time, and by the time we retired to bed in the early hours of the following morning, everyone was feeling the worse for wear.

I'd certainly had too much to drink, and although Graham is by no means a heavy drinker, he'd knocked back a fair few drams of his favourite malt whisky. For all that, he reminded me that the players would be going for a brisk walk at 10am, and invited me to join them.

Sheer pride made me turn up, wrapped in overcoat and scarf, for that morning walk with the players, when all I really wanted to do was climb back into bed and wait for the day to go away. I felt dreadful. It didn't help, either, when Graham turned up, looking as fit and fresh as ever, and greeted me with the words: "Morning Steve, you look bloody awful."

I didn't feel a whole lot better as I watched the match from the Directors' Box. Still feeling well and truly hung over, my mood wasn't even brightened by our 2-0 win. All I could do was keep staring down to the touchline, where Graham was constantly on his feet, yelling instructions at the players with all his usual enthusiasm. When it comes to holding your drink, footballers and coaches are clearly better equipped than club secretaries.

Another innovation introduced by Graham, after he had guided us to promotion at the first attempt, was his own version of meals on wheels. Deeply concerned about diet and meal patterns, particularly on match days, the last thing he wanted was for the players to go all day with next to nothing and then eat something heavy just before going to bed.

So whenever we played away, he would arrange for Erol Olcan from the Holiday Inn, to travel with us and prepare meals on the homeward journey. Because Erol was such a perfectionist, everything was done properly, with white tablecloths, silver service and three-course menus, but there was one rather restrictive problem.

Although the food had been prepared in advance, it had to be warmed in a microwave, which could only hold two or three meals at a time. This was all very well on long journeys from places like Newcastle, Norwich and Middlesbrough, but we frequently arrived back at Villa Park just as some of the players were tucking into their main course.

At least they weren't bored as they finished dining, because Graham always had plenty to say to them. Someone once suggested that Graham would never use a sentence to answer your question when a couple of hundred words would do, and there was never any question of him being lost for something to say, whether he was chatting to the players, the Press or the public.

I haven't come across a more talkative manager than Graham, although Gordon Lee comes a close second. The big difference is that where Taylor was always willing to listen to the other person's point of view, Lee didn't know when to button it. At least, that was the impression he gave when he was interviewed for the Villa job.

Gordon Lee, you may recall, was the man who had nothing to say on my behalf when he was scouting for Villa and saw me score a spectacular goal from the half-way line. I didn't remind him about his oversight when he came to the chairman's home to be considered as a successor to Tony Barton. Quite frankly, I never got the chance, and neither Doug Ellis nor director Tony Alderson were given much opportunity to make much input into the meeting, either.

Lee, a former Villa player, had a good pedigree as a manager by this stage of his career, having enjoyed considerable success in charge of Blackburn Rovers, Newcastle United and Everton, so he certainly seemed a strong candidate to take over at Villa Park.

If that was the case when he rang the doorbell at Doug Ellis's home, however, it certainly wasn't by the time we said goodbye later in the evening. Gordon Lee effectively talked himself out of the job.

The interview started promisingly enough. The chairman asked a straightforward question, inviting Lee to tell us why we should appoint him, and the answer initially made perfect sense. He had great affection for Villa, he said, having been there for years as a player, and had since gained a great deal of managerial experience with other big clubs.

So far, so good. Then he started to lose his way. Maybe it was nerves, maybe he was trying too hard to impress, but Lee droned on and on in his deep Black Country accent for the next couple of hours. By the time we broke up, myself, the chairman and Tony Alderson had all been close to nodding off at one stage or another. We decided not to appoint him. If he had this effect on us, what on earth would his team-talk be like? More to the point, would he ever have time to finish it before kick-off?

Chapter Nine

It's Just Not Cricket

The batsman braced himself as the next delivery came hurtling towards him. Without flickering an eyelid, he made solid contact to send his shot hurtling towards mid-off. Then, suddenly, he froze in horror. He had put too much height on the ball, and the fielder was perfectly positioned.

"Catch it, catch it!" screamed the bowler, anxious for his first wicket of the day. But it was too late. The fielder, looking totally bemused and not at all sure what he should be doing, let the ball slip through his fingers and on to the ground.

This scenario took place in July 1989, not at Lord's, The Oval or Edgbaston, but just outside Copenhagen. I was the batsman, Graham Taylor was the bowler, Norwegian agent Rune Hauge was the fielder – and there wasn't a bat or ball in sight! We did have an audience, however. Officials of FC Brøndby, watching from a nearby window, had never seen anything like our pretend game of cricket, and even Hauge, for all his astute financial mind, didn't really have a clue what was going on.

So perhaps I should explain just how the secretary and manager of Aston Villa became engaged in a game of pretend cricket with one of Europe's best-known football wheeler-dealers. I'm sure you're aware that football managers use all manner of tactics when it comes to the business of pursuing a prospective new signing. Quite apart from the financial inducements which a club may be offering the new boy, the manager has to convince the player he will be happy in his new surroundings, and that his wife or girlfriend will be made to feel at home.

Sometimes, though, the hardest part of arranging a deal can be the small matter of reaching agreement with the other club over the size of the transfer fee. Invariably, the selling club's valuation is much higher than the amount the buying club are willing to pay, so you tend to get a bit of psychology creeping into the negotiations. How often have you read about a transfer falling through because of a disagreement over price, only for the deal to go through a week or so later after some sort of compromise has been reached?

It's at times like these that manager needs all the composure of a poker player, and I never saw a better example of soccer kidology than when we signed Danish international defender Kent Nielsen in that summer of 1989. I will always remain convinced that we got our man at the right price because of our imaginary Test match!

Taylor had already duped the media into thinking he was interested in a Swedish player when he went to watch the Scandinavian "derby" clash against Denmark, but a couple of weeks later he came into my office and told me to pack my bags in readiness for a trip to Copenhagen the following day.

Graham picked me up at 6am to drive to Heathrow Airport for the flight, and on arrival in Denmark, we were met by Hauge, the man who was at the centre of the "bung" scandal which cost George Graham his job as manager of Arsenal a few years later. Rune took us first to our hotel, and then to the outskirts of Copenhagen, where the headquarters of Nielsen's club Brøndby are situated.

Many foreign clubs have their offices away from the stadium where they actually play, and in Brøndby's case, the administration operates from their training ground. It reminded me very much of an English rugby club, with a number of pitches surrounding a two-storey club-house which housed a committee room on one level and a bar and restaurant on the other.

When we got there, Hauge introduced us to Kent, and we discussed his terms, which appeared to present no problem. The stumbling block was the fee Brøndby wanted for him. They wanted £1m, we started talking around £200,000, knowing we were willing to go up to £500,000.

Having reached that figure, we made it clear we were unwilling to go any higher, while the Brøndby people were equally adamant they wanted more. Stalemate. When it became apparent neither club was willing to budge, there seemed little point in continuing the talks, so Graham played the first of his clever hands. He told them we were going home.

No, they said, why not wait outside while we discuss the situation among ourselves, and then we can talk again. So Graham, Rune and I went out into the Danish sunshine, and discovered that as well as all the football pitches, the Brøndby complex also boasted a cricket pitch.

If Taylor was getting concerned that his prospective new defender might slip through his grasp, he certainly wasn't about to show it. I don't think I've ever seen anyone quite so relaxed.

No sooner had we expressed our surprise at seeing a cricket field spread out before us, than Graham said: "Let's have a game." Never mind the fact that we not only had no equipment and were dressed in suits. I won the toss and elected to bat, requesting a middle and leg guard, Graham rubbed his imaginary cricket ball in readiness for the first over, at the same time instructing Rune where to stand in the field. Poor Rune just looked at us open-mouthed. Here we were, taking a break from negotiations over a major international transfer, and the manager and secretary of Aston Villa were acting like kids in a school playground

For the next five minutes or so, Graham went through the motion of bowling, I played the shots, and a bemused Rune went scurrying after the invisible ball. Then came the missed catch which earned our agent friend a telling-off, and prompted Graham to speed up his deliveries – whereupon he slipped and got his suit trousers covered in dust. Eventually, he got me out (bowled, of course, it was no use relying on Rune's fielding!) and took over at the crease as I delivered a few overs.

If Rune was confused by it all, the Brøndby officials watching from their window must have thought we had either gone totally crazy or had simply lost interest in the transfer deal. Either way, they asked us to go back in, told us they would accept our offer, and Nielsen was ours for £500,000. If the cricket had continued a little longer, we might even have got a reduction on the price!

As it was, Nielsen would arguably have been a decent buy even at the £1 million Brøndby originally asked, for he did a good job at the heart of the defence during his three years with the club. Along with Paul McGrath and Derek Mountfield, he helped to form the three-man back line which Graham introduced in a 2-0 win at Wimbledon (the old Plough Lane ground, not Selhurst Park) in November 1989 and which provided the backbone of our success that season. Although we finished well adrift of champions Liverpool, runners-up spot earned us a place in the following season's UEFA Cup, the first time an English club had been allowed to play in European competition since the Heysel Stadium disaster of 1985. I'm sure no Villa supporter will ever forget, either, the tremendous long-range goal he scored against Inter Milan on the night we humbled the Italian giants 2-0 at Villa Park.

Quite apart from his football talents, though, Kent was also a thoroughly nice guy, and someone who was determined to get the most from his time in England. Kent, who speaks perfect English, was never less than courteous during his time with the club, whether he was speaking to the chairman or chatting to supporters outside the ground, and he and his lovely wife Karen couldn't get enough of our culture, visiting places like Stratford and Warwick whenever the chance arose. They also became good friends of my wife Carolyn and I, and we frequently went out for dinner together. Like me, Kent is also a big music fan, and he loves the Electric Light Orchestra. I once arranged for him to meet Jeff Lynne and he was absolutely thrilled to have his photograph taken with ELO's lead singer – just like a young Villa supporter would have been excited at having a photo taken with Kent. Players obviously come and go over the years, and you accept it is part of the business, but I have to confess I was sorry to see Kent return to Denmark and join Aarhus early in 1992.

If an imaginary game of cricket contributed to landing Kent's signature for Villa, perhaps we should have tried a spot of French Cricket when we signed Didier Six from Mulhouse a few years earlier. Six will go down in Aston Villa history as the first French player to join the club, although looking back on the events leading up to his debut, I'm still amazed the transfer ever came to fruition. It all started promisingly enough, with a phone call from Michel Verschuren, the general manager of Belgian club Anderlecht, who we had beaten in the 1982 European Cup semi-final.

Michel informed me that Anderlecht had the chance to sign Six, whose French club had been relegated the previous season, but they already had their full complement of foreign players. The midfielder had subsequently indicated an interest in playing in England, and because of the close relationship between Anderlecht and Villa, Verschuren had decided to alert us to a player who had played 52 times for France, including the 1978 and 1982 World Cups and the 1984 European Championships.

Six also had a solid domestic pedigree, having previously been with Lens, Marseilles and Strasbourg in his home country as well as having spells with Bruges in Belgium and Stuttgart in Germany, so we agreed that he could join us in training for a couple of weeks. Graham Turner, our manager at the time, liked what he saw, and by Tuesday, October 2, 1982, negotiations between the clubs had been completed. The boy Didier was duly introduced to the media at Villa Park, and was pencilled in for his debut against Manchester United the following Saturday. Sounds simple, doesn't it? You must be joking! I seemed to spend the next couple of days chasing all over Europe to tie up the loose ends of the deal and ensure that everything was in order.

When transactions take place between clubs from different countries, you have to be absolutely sure there are no errors on any of the documents. The slightest discrepancy has to be ironed out, and if there does happen to be a mistake, any alterations have to be signed, not only by representatives of both clubs, but by the player, too. There was something I wanted to check on Six's International Clearance Certificate, so arrangements were made for me to fly from Birmingham to Paris on the Wednesday to collect the certificate from the French Football Federation headquarters. While in Paris, I was also due to meet the Mulhouse president to collect the signed agreement between the two clubs, which was required by the Football League by 5pm on Thursday to ensure that our new star could line up against United.

All of this appeared to be quite straightforward, until my arrangements were thrown into chaos by a call on the Tuesday evening saying I would have to go to Mulhouse the following day because their president was unable to be in Paris. I could have climbed the Eiffel Tower in frustration. Instead of a simple flight to the French capital, the new arrangements meant I had to drive to Heathrow, and then catch a plane to Basle, the nearest airport to Mulhouse, which is near the French-Swiss border. Stuart Webb, of the Derby-based Lonsdale Travel, even had to go to his office at 10.30 that night to arrange *tickets on departure* for my new schedule.

To add to the confusion, I had earlier tried to contact a Football Association official for advice over the query I had on the International Clearance Certificate. I won't embarrass the fellow by naming him, but it has to be said he was rather less than helpful. When I phoned his home I quickly explained the problem to his wife, insisting that I wouldn't take more than a minute of his time. She told me to hang on a minute while she called him. I couldn't believe it when she returned and informed me: "He's washing his hair, ring him after nine in the morning" – and put down the receiver.

This wasn't exactly what I wanted to hear when I was already pre-occupied with altering travel arrangements and trying to make sure the deal was not delayed because of any oversight on my part. The matter on which I wanted clarification was not a major issue, but having failed to get an answer from the FA man who was busy with his shampoo, I did a fair bit of tossing and turning before my alarm woke me at 5am the following day.

After an hour's wait at Basle Airport, I was met by Mulhouse officials and Didier's business partner Gilbert Leinhard, with whom I had lunch before I eventually got to see the club president at around 4.30pm. After a couple of hours of discussions, I then travelled to Paris in a small plane which flew at cloud level, and felt decidedly unwell as the aircraft was buffeted by turbulence throughout one of the most uncomfortable journeys I've encountered.

At least I could content myself with the fact that the documents I needed from Mulhouse were in my possession. All I had to do now was lodge them with the French Football Federation and return with them to Britain so that Didier could be registered by the Thursday afternoon deadline.

The FFF, unfortunately, were barely any more helpful than the FA man who had declined to come to the telephone. I reported to their headquarters early on the Thursday morning, handed over the papers, and after a long wait I was told everything was in order – and that the documents would be posted to me. This, of course, was of no use whatsoever when the papers needed to be at the Football League's offices in Lytham St Annes by the same afternoon.

It was time to take a firm hand. Using my best pidgin French, I pleaded with the French officials to let me take the forms back with me, explaining that without them, Didier would not be able to play against Manchester United that Saturday. The impression I got was that our French friends couldn't care less whether Didier played or not, but after a great deal of chuntering, they reluctantly agreed.

After a frantic taxi ride to Charles De Gaulle airport, I just managed to catch the 12.30 flight to Heathrow, and by 3.45pm I arrived at the Football Association headquarters in Lancaster Gate. By this time, it was just an hour and a quarter to deadline, and despite all my endeavours of the past couple of days, it crossed my mind that something might still go wrong, and I would be blamed for Didier's transfer not being registered soon enough for him to make his debut.

It seemed to take an eternity as the papers were faxed to Lytham for approval, but in reality the whole business must have taken about half an hour. By 4.15, the forms were returned to London, and with 45 minutes to spare, Six was clear to play against United.

Villa Park has witnessed some stunning debuts down the years, and Didier Six's performance on October 6, 1984 ranks among the best. He crowned a brilliant individual display by laying on a goal for Peter Withe in our 2-1 win, and I had a great feeling of satisfaction as I watched from the Directors' Box, knowing I had played my part in making sure our new signing could play.

Needless to say the media had a field day. *"United hit by Six Of The Best"*, *"Vive Le Withe as slick Six clicks"* and *"United get a French lesson"* were just some of the headlines which screamed across the sports pages the following morning.

Sadly, things went downhill from there. Didier never really settled in this country, starting only 13 games in a Villa shirt, and it was no real surprise when he returned across the Channel the following summer to join Metz. In fairness, the fact that he didn't speak much English didn't really help. The club's Share Registrar Bert Sisk helped out with translation whenever Didier was in the club offices, but our players, with the exception of Allan Evans, didn't really want to know. Football is supposed to be an international language, but Didier simply didn't fit in.

If that was one example of a foreign signing not working out, we had an even better one six years later. In years to come, I can imagine the question popping up during a sports quiz: Which Aston Villa player scored an important goal for the club without ever playing for them?

No doubt the majority of Villa fans will be aware that I'm talking about Ivo Stas, the midfielder who joined us from Slovakian club Banik Ostrava in November, 1990, the month after we had beaten Banik in the first round of the UEFA Cup.

The goal Stas scored for Villa was, in fact, an own goal in our 2-1 second leg victory, but apart from that slip, he played well enough to suggest he would be a useful addition to our squad, particularly as we were managed at the time by the former Czechoslovakian national coach Jo Venglos. Senior players like Gordon Cowans, Paul McGrath and David Platt were in full agreement with Jo that Stas would be a beneficial acquisition, and the general consensus was that at £500,000 we were getting a player who would have cost three times as much in this country. Unfortunately, the theory was never tested. Almost as soon as he arrived, Stas was laid low by an Achilles tendon injury, and spent the rest of the season keeping physio Jim Walker company in the treatment room instead of displaying his "libero" talents just in front of our defenders.

By the start of the following season it became evident that Stas would have to give up professional football. He did manage to turn out in a couple of pre-season friendlies, including one in Hanover in which he looked promising, but not long afterwards he was on a plane back home and Villa were collecting compensation on what must surely rate as the saddest signing in the club's history. Like Didier Six before him, Stas never felt at home in a foreign country, although in this case, the blame lay firmly at the player's own door.

I don't think I ever heard Stas utter more than a dozen words during his spell with us. Perhaps I should have been forewarned when he was so quiet during our contract negotiations with him, although I put that down to an initial shyness with strangers, and the fact that Jo Venglos was able to do all the talking for him.

The signing of Stas wasn't quite as fraught as when I had to chase all over France and Switzerland to tie up the Six deal, but it still involved three days in Prague for myself, chairman Doug Ellis and Dr Jo. On our first night in the city, Stas and Banik's general manager Jan Pavliska came to our hotel, and everything was pretty straightforward as we agreed a contract which, including a two-year option, was designed to make Ivo a Villa player until the end of the 1994-95 season. During the course of the following day, however, we had to complete one document after another before the transfer could be completed. I reckon we signed at least 10 forms, and that was even before we got to the English ones.

Seems a lot of trouble, doesn't it, for someone who would never kick a ball for the club in a competitive match? Still, Ivo's lack of action earned him a certain notoriety among Holte Enders, and the Villa fanzine *Heroes and Villans* even conjured up a regular column called *"Ivo Writes Home"*. The spoof letters were amusing enough, but what he actually wrote in correspondence to the folks back in Ostrava, I shudder to think.

Chapter Ten

Things We Said Today

On Merseyside, they filed downstairs to The Cavern; in Birmingham we climbed the stairs to The Carlton. All right, so the Brummie version doesn't have quite the same magical ring. Yet my regular Sunday night haunt of the Swinging Sixties can't have been so far removed from what later became a world famous Liverpool landmark.

The Beatles, the Cavern's most illustrious inhabitants, never played at The Carlton. But the smoky, sweaty room, located above a furniture store in Erdington High Street, did provide a platform for some of Britain's biggest pop names. The Who, Cream and Rod Stewart all performed there in their early days, and I saw them all. Mind you, I had to perfect the art of walking on tiptoes as I passed the bouncers on the door, before I reached my 18th birthday and could legally enter the building.

If I had been aware of the potential dangers of the place, maybe I wouldn't have been quite so keen to gain admission, big names or not. One night I turned up early to see a lesser-known group, Simon Dupree and The Big Sound, and I was fascinated to watch them setting up their equipment. It was something of an eye-opener when I noticed that one of the sockets they were were using had something like 15 extension leads plugged into it. Without being an electrical genius, it occurred to me that this might be an overload situation. Still, these guys obviously knew what they were doing. They'd even had a record called *Kites* in the Top Ten.

I'm surprised everyone in the audience wasn't blown as high as kites when Dupree and his pals launched into their set. They had barely played a note when there was an almighty explosion, followed by a puff of smoke as the room was plunged into total darkness. They may have been up-and-coming pop stars, but their knowledge of matters electrical was clearly limited. They had fused the whole building.

Despite that unfortunate incident, my enthusiasm for the music scene never wavered, and is still as strong as ever today. When I get away from my desk at Villa Park, there's nothing I enjoy more than popping a CD into the player and putting my feet up. In my humble opinion, there's no better way of relaxing. I love browsing in record shops, too, and I hate to think how much of my hard-earned cash has been spent on vinyl, cassette and compact disc.

When it comes to rock music, I'm a bit of a fanatic, never happier than when exciting new sounds are blasting through the speakers. My tastes are pretty varied, too, and I'm one of those people who often buys a record after reading a good review in a music magazine.

My first record purchase, I have to admit, was rather more calculated. In 1959, I saved my pocket money for weeks in order to buy a single which featured in the pop charts for 25 weeks. If I was trying to impress you with my impeccable musical taste from a very early age, I suppose I could say it was something by a rock legend like Elvis Presley or Buddy Holly. I would be lying. The single which launched my record collection was Emile Ford and the Checkmates singing *What Do You Want To Make Those Eyes At Me For?*

A few years passed before I delved into what was considered the more meaningful business of buying LPs. The first album to find its way onto my turntable was *The Five Faces of Manfred Mann*, a record I bought after I'd been to see the group at Blackpool's North Pier theatre during a family holiday. Mum, dad and my older sister Christine went to that particular concert, which also featured Birmingham's Spencer Davis Group, at my insistence. It was, however, a choice I came to regret. For some strange reason I've never been able to explain, I opted for that show when we could just as easily have gone to see the Beatles at the ABC Theatre.

Possibly it was because my parents, like so many people of their age, had begun to enjoy the Fab Four's music. Rather than being pleased that they actually shared my taste, I engaged in a touch of teenage rebellion by insisting we go to watch two groups who were not so popular. Anyway, I paid a heavy price. The Beatles were my idols, but I never did get to see them perform live.

The nearest I came was when our next door neighbour, a cameraman at ATV, got us studio tickets when John, Paul, George and Ringo were top of the bill on the pop programme *Thank Your Lucky Stars*. On the day the show was recorded I went down with flu, and although Dad and Chris took me along to the ATV studios in Birmingham, I was so ill I just couldn't go in.

Still, at least I have a few prized souvenirs of my music heroes. In addition to every record they ever made, plus a few bootlegs, I also have the autographs of the best pop group in music history. These were obtained for me by Lilian Swain, wife of Kenny Swain, who was a member of Villa's European Cup-winning side. Lilian helped to run The Beatles' fan club in their early days, and knew them quite well. She also gave me a card which was sent to her one Christmas, signed by "the boys".

Apart from listening to music I also enjoy playing the guitar, and I've built up quite a collection of plectrums, thanks mainly to friends within the music industry, such as Walsall-based concert promoter Tim Parsons and Phil Hatton, who looks after the interests of ELO's Jeff Lynne in this country. Both Tim and Phil are avid Villa supporters, and have been only too willing to help my collection along.

Among the "famous" plectrums I've acquired are those belonging to Lynne, Mark Knopfler, Eric Clapton, George Harrison, Black Sabbath's Geezer Butler, and Hank Marvin. But the one which stands out above them all is Paul McCartney's – even if I can't claim that it has improved my own strumming. The audience for my guitar picking is usually restricted to my immediate family, wife Carolyn and children Lucy, Matthew and Jack, although I did once make a public appearance.

At Villa's Christmas party a couple of years ago, I was persuaded to get up on stage with a local group called Swains – featuring a sports journalist friend of mine, Martin Swain – plus violin virtuoso Nigel Kennedy. We played two Beatles songs, *Things We Said Today* and *I Saw Her Standing There,* before manager Ron Atkinson joined us for his rendition of *My Way*. If my memory serves me correctly, there were no calls for an encore as I returned to my seat. Still, at least I can claim to have played alongside a man whose violin playing is admired worldwide and a group who have since produced an excellent four-track compact disc.

Over the years, my job has brought me into contact with countless pop and showbiz celebrities, including Eric Morecambe, Eric Sykes, Mick Hucknall, Robert Plant, Kate Bush, Robbie Williams and Tom Watt, better known as Lofty in the TV soap *EastEnders*, who have all been guests at Villa matches. I also renewed my acquaintance with Rod Stewart when he performed an open air concert at Villa Park, having met him more than a decade earlier when I was invited to be a judge at a beauty contest.

That was the year after we had played Valur in the European Cup. It turned out that one of their directors, Baldvin Jonson, was also involved in organising the Miss Iceland competition, and I was delighted when he asked me to be a member of the judging panel. I was even more ecstatic when I discovered I would be sitting alongside Stewart, who was out there to watch his beloved Scotland football team play Iceland.

It was a wonderful night. Myself, Rod and the other members of the panel clearly made the right selection, because the girl we chose went on to become Miss World, although I was really more interested in chatting to one of the biggest names in the music business, and listening to his impromptu 20-minute performance. When we left the nightclub at 2.30am, it was still light – at certain times of the year Iceland does not experience darkness because of its close proximity to the Arctic Circle – and we wandered down to the harbour for breakfast at one of the quaint little cafes along the quayside.

Elton John is another rock superstar I've met twice. Having seen him something like a dozen times in concert, it was strange sitting next to him when he came to Villa Park for a meeting in his capacity as chairman of Watford. He also made a point of coming over to say hello to Carolyn and I when I took her to a Villa match at Vicarage Road during the time she was pregnant with our first child, Lucy. For all his outgoing personality on stage, he came across as a rather nervous person, who went out of his way to be polite.

The same can hardly be said of Villa's most famous supporter. Nigel Kennedy has developed an outlandish image which, despite his brilliant playing, has made him something of a rebel among the classical music fraternity. He's no different in his private life, either. No matter who he is addressing, the chances are his opening gambit will be "Hiya, Monster". Nigel is also the only person I know who dares to call the chairman "Deadly" to his face.

Kennedy's affection for the club became public knowledge in the late 1970s, when he appeared on a music awards ceremony on television. He received his award with the words: "This is nearly as big a thrill as watching Aston Villa win the League Cup."

Bert Sisk, our Share Registrar, saw the programme, and subsequently wrote to Nigel, asking if he would like to attend a game as our guest. Since then, I can't think of another club who have such a devoted celebrity supporter. Nigel has followed the team to all parts of the country in his Jaguar – which he has aptly sprayed in claret-and-blue graffiti – and has also accompanied us to various matches abroad.

Wherever he goes, too, he is asked to give a performance, and he invariably obliges. Boardrooms nationwide have resounded to the sweet sound of his violin, and he also performed an "open air" concert when we were in Milan for a UEFA Cup-tie in 1994, on the roof terrace of the British Consulate.

Our zany superstar fan, who served for three years as a senior vice-president of the club, frequently broke Directors' Box protocol on his early visits. He never wore a tie, and knowing his laid-back approach to life, I'm not sure he even owned one. He turned up for one match with a bootlace around his neck, and another with a silk scarf, which he proudly exhibited for the visiting directors in our guest lounge.

"This was worn by Jimi Hendrix at the Isle of Wight Festival," he told them. "There, look, that's where his blood dried on it. I've never washed it in case it comes off." Our guests, having earlier delighted in Nigel's playing, were rather less impressed by this story of a rock legend.

But that's Nigel Kennedy. You take him as you find him, and if his lack of respect for the establishment offends you, well, that's tough. While he is undeniably nonconformist, however, his affection for Villa is beyond question. He has even arranged concert dates, both in this country and overseas, to fit in with our fixtures. And whenever he has to miss games, he is invariably on the phone within minutes of the final whistle to check out the result. I don't know much about the violin, but I wouldn't mind betting his audience are treated to a more inspired performance after a Villa victory.

Unlike many other celebrity supporters, who I'm sure would not be quite so enthusiastic without the guarantee of a complimentary ticket, Nigel is a genuine fan. All that matters to him is watching the team play, regardless of the price of admission or the comfort of the surroundings. He was never happier than when he stood on the Holte End before our ground was transformed into an all-seater stadium.

Nigel even campaigned for terraces to be retained, organising a petition among our supporters, and I don't think anyone was more disappointed when the all-seater proposal of Lord Justice Taylor's post-Hillsborough report came into effect. Give him the choice, and Nigel would much rather be chanting and singing behind the goal than sitting demurely in the Directors' Box.

As for myself, if my guitar playing is never going to turn me into a rock megastar, at least I've been able to try my hand as a promoter. I had no involvement with Rod Stewart's Villa Park concert, nor the one by Bruce Springsteen in 1988 for that matter, but I can claim to have organised a couple of small gigs.

The idea occurred to me after I had been to a couple of concerts in Wolverhampton, where former members of big-name groups performed with the accompaniment of just their own guitar. Glen Tilbrook, former lead singer with Squeeze, sowed the seed in my mind when he created a wonderful atmosphere at the unlikely setting of the Connaught Hotel. And after seeing Ray Davies of the Kinks in a similar setting at the Wulfrun Hall, I found myself thinking: "Why do I have to drive 20 miles to Wolverhampton for this sort of entertainment?"

The answer was that Birmingham, supposedly England's Second City, had no venue suitable for such an intimate concert. No disrespect to Tilbrook or Davies, but I couldn't see them creating much of an atmosphere inside the NEC Arena or the city's new Symphony Hall.

Suddenly it dawned on me where I could find a venue for this type of concert – my place of work. That was how *Villa Park Unplugged* was launched, and the first two gigs were both sell-outs, albeit with a capacity limited to 160.

The project was launched by local singer Micky Greaney, who has played to sell-out audiences at Ronnie Scott's Jazz Club in Birmingham, and he was followed by Steve Harley, leader of the 1970s group Cockney Rebel. All right, so the North Stand Banqueting Suite doesn't sound quite as magical as The Cavern, nor even The Carlton, come to think of it. But at least I no longer have to stand on tiptoes to get in!

Chapter Eleven

Sheffield Wednesday, Villa Thursday

The balmy Spring afternoon was perfect for a football match. A shirt-sleeved crowd of over 46,000 had assembled at Villa Park, and the stage was set for the FA Cup semi-final between Everton and Norwich City. As always on semi-final days, there was hope and optimism in the air, an eager anticipation from both sets of supporters that their teams were just one match away from Wembley and English football's most glamorous match of all, the FA Cup Final.

Even though my own club were not involved, I shared that feeling of contentment as I settled down in the Directors' Box. This was the 11th time my duties had required me to organise Villa's hosting of a semi-final, and the task no longer filled me with the dread it had in my early days as club secretary. Granted, there was still a nagging concern that everything might not go to plan, but over the years semi-final day had become less and less stressful.

On this particular day things could hardly have gone any better. The weather was perfect, both sets of supporters were in good voice, and everyone was looking forward to an enjoyable Cup-tie between two of the country's most attractive footballing teams.

But please don't ask me to relate any details of that 90 minutes. The record books show that Pat Nevin's goal gave Everton a 1-0 victory, but beyond that I can't help you. Almost as soon as the match kicked off, Adrian Titcombe, the Football Association's Head of Competitions, informed us there was a problem at the other semi-final between Liverpool and Nottingham Forest at Hillsborough.

The game, he said, had been stopped because of crowd congestion behind one of the goals. Suddenly, everyone's thoughts were concentrated on what was happening 90 miles away in Sheffield, rather than the action taking place in front of us at Villa Park. Initial reports from Hillsborough were sketchy, but there was a suggestion that someone had died in a crush at the Leppings Lane End. Then it was two people, then 10. Eventually, the grim statistic rose to 96.

April 15, 1989, will always be remembered as the blackest day in English football, the day that even people with absolutely no interest in the game were shocked and stunned by the horrific events of Hillsborough. I'm not ashamed to say I cried that night, my tears reflecting a mixture of grief and relief.

Watching *Match of the Day's* eerie coverage of the tragedy on BBC, it seemed unbelievable that such horrific events could happen at a football ground in this country. My own emotion was heightened by the fact I had been instrumental in organising the day's other semi-final – and even more so by the knowledge that I might easily have been right at the heart of the Hillsborough Disaster. It was a sobering thought, indeed, that less than three years earlier I had been on the brink of joining Sheffield Wednesday, and only an 11th hour change of heart had prevented me from heading up the M1 to assume the role of secretary of the South Yorkshire club.

Very much like a player who has come up through the ranks and seen big-money signings receive all the accolades, I had begun to feel unsettled at Villa Park towards the end of 1986. It had been seven years since my appointment as secretary, and somehow there was a feeling, possibly not correct but real enough in my own mind, that I was no longer appreciated.

I'm the sort of guy who thrives on encouragement, and likes an arm around the shoulder from time to time, and it no longer seemed to be happening.

Maybe this was because I was regarded as efficient in the job, and responsible enough to get on with it in my own way, but there was still a nagging worry at the back of my mind that I was being taken for granted. So when Dick Chester telephoned to say he was leaving the post of Sheffield Wednesday secretary to form his own financial consultancy, my interest was immediately aroused. Dick's inquiry was along the lines of "Do you know anyone who might be interested in the job?" He obviously caught me on a day when I was a bit down in the dumps, because I immediately replied: "Yes, me."

I soon found myself believing Wednesday might be the perfect move, too. After all, I had always regarded them as very much like Villa in terms of facilities and stature, and the more I thought about it, the more a "transfer" to Hillsborough appealed to me.

Things progressed pretty quickly after Dick had sensed I was serious. Wednesday chairman Bert McGhee phoned me at home, and the next thing I knew I was sitting at his home one Sunday afternoon, talking over my proposed move. It wasn't so much an interview, more a case of " When can you start?" Without wishing to sound big-headed, I suppose Wednesday were more than happy at the prospect of recruiting someone who had been secretary of a League Championship and European Cup-winning club within the previous five years.

Anyway, I returned home, talked things over with my wife Carolyn, and decided to go for it. And almost as soon as I had taken the decision, I started to regret it. For starters, there was the business of telling the chairman I was leaving, a task I didn't fancy one bit. Worse, much to my surprise, he seemed genuinely devastated by the news, stressing how strongly he valued my services. We had barely finished one of the most difficult conversations of my life when the seeds of doubt began to set in.

Still, the decision had been taken, and they say you should never look back in these situations. That's easier said than done, as I'm sure anyone who has ever contemplated a career change will appreciate. Over the next two or three weekends, Carolyn and I drove to Sheffield on numerous occasions, looking for somewhere to live, but no matter how hard we searched, we could find nowhere which appealed as much as our own Sutton Coldfield district of Birmingham. Wednesday even arranged for their manager Howard Wilkinson's wife to show us the more desirable parts of South Yorkshire, including an area called Dore. It was more attractive than most of the other places we went house-hunting, but deep down we knew it wasn't where we wanted to spend the rest of our lives.

As the search continued in earnest, things were also moving on the job front. I was in the process of serving my notice at Villa, and arrangements were made for me to spend one day a week at Hillsborough, to become accustomed to Wednesday's way of working. In the event, the arrangement lasted all of one day - ironically a Wednesday.

If you had spent that day with me, you probably wouldn't have seen any reason for a change of heart. It was simply a case of "shadowing" Dick Chester, and starting to learn his methods of working, which were not a great deal different from my own. All the Wednesday staff were friendly, and a reporter from Radio Sheffield called in to interview me about my appointment.There was even a social aspect to the day, a farewell cocktail party for a director who was leaving the club, so I had the chance to meet the other Board members over a drink.

If all of this sounds like a very pleasant and gentle introduction to a new job, I certainly can't deny it. Wednesday were going out of their way to make sure I felt welcome. They were a nice bunch of people, and there was absolutely no reason why I was unlikely to get along with them.

Yet as I was driving home that evening, the thought struck me right between the eyes: "What on earth am I doing?" While a switch to Sheffield was appealing, my mind was suddenly flooded with reasons why I shouldn't be making such a move. My wife was pregnant, she was upset at the thought of leaving Birmingham, we hadn't found anywhere to live in Yorkshire, Carolyn's mother was seriously ill.

All of these factors began to torment me during that homeward drive, and then came the clincher. Once I had parted company with Villa, the club would replace me and there would be no going back. By handing in my notice, I had started something which was rapidly getting beyond my control. What was I doing, leaving a great club like Aston Villa? I had supported them all my life, I was settled in the job, and the chairman had made it clear he didn't want to lose me.

Carolyn looked inquiringly at me as I walked through the door, wondering how the day had gone. I told her simply: "I'm making a big mistake." The words were music to her ears, because right from the start she hadn't been keen on moving away from the Midlands. But it wasn't that straightforward.

I might have changed my mind, Carolyn might have been delighted, but for all I knew, my Villa days may already have been over. The chairman obviously had to find a replacement, and may well have done so while I had been pre-occupied with my new job. Or he may have reached the conclusion that once I had stated my intention to leave, there should be no reversal of that decision.

My heart was thumping as I dialled Doug Ellis's home phone number, knowing my U-turn had possibly come too late. It was like someone else was saying the words as I told him I had changed my mind and wanted to stay at Villa, and nervously awaited his reaction. Thankfully, my fears were unfounded. Mr Ellis was, to quote an over-used football cliche, "over the moon".

No, he hadn't found a replacement and yes, the job was still mine. Then he snapped the instructions down the line: "Get changed, get yourself and Carolyn over here, and we'll crack open a bottle of champagne." That was the most enjoyable drop of bubbly I've ever tasted, and the four of us – myself, Carolyn, Mr Ellis and his wife Heidi – rounded off the evening by going out for dinner at the Lea Gardens Chinese Restaurant in Sutton Coldfield. There was still another difficult telephone call to be made, of course, the one informing Bert McGhee of my decision. This was something I didn't relish one bit because I felt I had let him down. It also meant Wednesday had to start searching for a new secretary all over again.

To be fair to Mr McGhee, he masked his disappointment and wished me all the best, and I have to say that on all my subsequent visits to Hillsborough, there has never been the slightest hint of animosity towards me. At least Luton Town's secretary Graham Mackrell was happy to hear I was staying at Villa. He was the man who took the Sheffield job, and we have become particularly good friends over the years.

One thing I would like to put on record is the fact that staying at Villa Park had nothing to do with money. At the time, a lot of people suggested I had been persuaded not to leave by the offer of a huge salary increase, but that wasn't the case at all. On the evening I decided Sheffield wasn't for me, Mr Ellis was so delighted that he offered to let me write out my own contract, but it was an offer I declined. I was happy enough knowing I was still secretary of the club which had always been closest to my heart. The next day I was back at my desk, feeling comfortable and very much where I belonged. It was a case of Sheffield Wednesday, Villa Thursday – and every other day of the week for that matter. Football may have come home to England during the 1996 European Championship Finals, but I did it a decade earlier.

Frank Spencer and David Baddiel recruiting for their Fantasy League team?

Chapter Twelve

Not So Deadly

He's served in the navy, played football for Southport, and has had business interests which have spanned travel, building and farming. But there is absolutely no question about where Doug Ellis's heart lies. He is obsessed with bringing success to Aston Villa. His whole life is devoted to the club, and every waking minute is dedicated to the cause. It wouldn't surprise me if he dreams in claret and blue.

Villa's chairman has had his fair share of criticism during his years at the helm, but he has made the club more shipshape, correct and financially sound than at any time in its history. And just where he gets his boundless energy and stamina, I simply don't know. I'm his junior by more than a quarter of a century, yet while I often feel exhausted at the end of a busy day, he frequently calls into my office to say he's just off to yet another function.

Even when he gets involved in matters outside the club, either as chairman of Sutton Coldfield's Good Hope Hospital, a member of the Football Association Council or chairman of the FA's Technical Control Board, he never lets it be forgotten that he is from Aston Villa. Quite simply, the club couldn't have a better ambassador.

A self-made millionaire, Doug Ellis has used his business prowess to transform Villa from a famous but relatively small-time club into one of modern football's genuine giants. You only have to look at some of the transfer fees we have paid in the last decade to see what I mean. When Graham Taylor took over as manager, just after we were relegated in 1987, his first two signings were Steve Sims from Watford for £50,000 and David Hunt on a free transfer. By the summer of 1996, we were splashing out £4m to Bolton Wanderers for Serbian midfielder Sasa Curcic, and 12 months earlier we had been willing to spend considerably more than that.

People sometimes accuse Doug of failing to compete with the likes of Manchester United, Liverpool and Newcastle United in the transfer market, but that's simply not the case. I'm sure we will be well into the next century before Villa contemplate spending £15m on a single player, as Newcastle did when they made Alan Shearer a world record signing. But that doesn't mean we lack ambition.

Before the start of the 1995-96 campaign, we sanctioned £9m worth of transfers for manager Brian Little, who brought in Gareth Southgate, Savo Milosevic and Mark Draper, and the figure could easily have been much higher. At £3.5m, Milosevic was our record signing at the time, but we had earlier tabled a £6m offer to Queens Park Rangers for England international Les Ferdinand.

In the event, Ferdinand decided to join Newcastle United, but not before we had made strenuous attempts to bring him to Villa Park. He came to the ground one Saturday morning to meet the chairman, the manager and myself, and made no secret of the fact he was impressed by the club. What didn't help was the fact we had only just avoided relegation the previous season, and although he had no qualms about the deal he was offered, Les felt he had more chance of winning something at St James Park. It was a decision we reluctantly had to accept, and a lot of Villa fans are convinced we might have become champions that season had Ferdinand joined us. Such is the irony of football though, that Newcastle won nothing, while we lifted the Coca-Cola Cup with the help of a superb Milosevic goal at Wembley.

Ferdinand wasn't the only big name we pursued that summer. In different circumstances, Paul Gascoigne might well have become a Villa player, but from the moment we expressed an interest, we were aware it was going to be an uphill battle to get him.

Gazza had already made it clear he fancied joining Glasgow Rangers when his contract with Italians Lazio came to an end, but that didn't stop Doug Ellis from making a bold bid to lure him into a claret-and-blue shirt. He had entertained Gascoigne and a few of England's other players on his yacht during the 1990 World Cup in Italy, and had always liked the idea of bringing such a high-profile player to the club.

When the chairman and I met the former Newcastle and Tottenham star's agent Mel Stein at his weekend retreat in the heart of the Cotswolds, we were told Gascoigne would definitely be leaving Italy, but that a number of clubs, including Rangers, had expressed a strong interest. Straight away, we knew we faced fierce competition, and when Stein told us the financial package Gazza was seeking, it was far and away above what we had ever paid an Aston Villa player.

Nevertheless, Doug said he was willing to find out what the player wanted. Even though the indications were that Gascoigne had set his heart on joining the Scottish champions, the chairman refused to let the matter rest. The odds may have been against him, but he certainly wasn't going to give in without a fight, and we made plans to fly out to Rome.

If the answer was to be no, the chairman wanted to hear it straight from the horse's mouth. He was still aggrieved about a potential signing which had gone wrong a few years earlier, when Neil Webb had indicated he would be joining us from Portsmouth. Webb told us that as a matter of courtesy, he first had to to talk to Nottingham Forest, and the chairman reluctantly agreed. The next thing we knew, Forest manager Brian Clough had persuaded him to go to the City Ground. It was very much a case of once bitten, twice shy. Since that abortive deal, any player agreeing a move to Villa is not allowed to leave the chairman's office until he has signed his contract.

This was a slightly different situation, because Gazza hadn't said he wanted to come to Villa, but I could sense Doug was summoning all his powers of persuasion as we flew to Rome. Right from the start though, the odds seemed to be stacked against us.

Gascoigne was supposed to phone us at the Hilton Hotel to arrange a meeting over dinner, but the call never came. Later in the evening, to be fair, we were informed that his absence was unavoidable because a friend had been involved in a serious car crash, and Gazza was at his bedside in hospital.

Our meeting was re-arranged for the following morning, and this time Gascoigne turned up on time, accompanied by his famous "minder", Jimmy *Five Bellies* Gardner. I went down to meet them in reception, and took Gazza and his portly pal up to the chairman's room so we could talk in private. He may be a millionaire, but there are no airs and graces about this Geordie boy. The first thing he and *Five Bellies* did was to help themselves to what was left of Doug's breakfast.

Then the talking started, the chairman extolling the virtues of Aston Villa while Gascoigne kept stressing his preference for Rangers. On reflection, I suppose we were always on a loser. Here was one of the world's top players making a decision about his future. Should he join a team who had just won the Scottish championship for the umpteenth time and qualified for the European Champions League, or one who had narrowly escaped the dreaded drop from the Premiership? Well, what would you do?

"Sorry Dugg," said Gazza eventually in his distinctive Geordie accent. "You're a great bloke, you've got a great club, and I have the highest regard for your manager. But I've promised Rangers I'll talk to them again."

Once the hard talking was over, and the chairman had grudgingly conceded he would not be making the quick signing he wanted, we chatted for a while, and I took a photograph of Gazza on the balcony for a souvenir. Typical of how the meeting had gone, the film was over-exposed, and my picture never saw the light of day. I did, however, get his autograph on one of my business cards to take home for my son Matthew, so I can at least claim to have succeeded where the chairman failed – by getting Paul Gascoigne's signature!

Had we succeeded in landing Gascoigne and Ferdinand, who knows what our total outlay would have been during that close season? Those two alone would have cost around £10m, and although we would then have saved on the Milosevic and Draper deals, I'm sure Brian Little would still have signed Southgate. That would have taken the club's outlay between seasons to a cool £12.5m.

The chairman would happily have funded such major transfer activity too, although he wasn't always in a position to contemplate such a grand spending spree. He has accumulated his wealth by following that simple but sensible policy of looking after the pennies. When I first joined the club, Doug was still involved with his travel business, and it was usually well into the afternoon before he called in at the ground. Invariably, he would go round switching off any lights he felt were unnecessary, and telling us off for being wasteful. This used to amuse the staff, but no-one can dispute the fact that such a thrifty approach has yielded rich long-term dividends for Aston Villa. To this day, in fact, everyone at the ground thinks twice before flicking a light switch.

At least Doug was being careful with the club's money. Another Villa chairman, Ron Bendall, clearly didn't like spending his own. Bendall, a multi-millionaire, lived as a tax exile on the Isle of Man, which meant there were only a limited number of days he could spend in mainland Britain. This suited everyone at the club, because no-one was particularly fond of him. Whenever he came over he would park himself in my office and let forth with a stream of the corniest, dirtiest jokes I'd ever heard. Most of them weren't even funny, but I had to laugh along with him, just to be polite.

Early one evening, during a chat with his wife, I discovered that the chairman was as tight with his cash as he was free with his appalling jokes. It was around 6.10pm, and most of the staff had gone home, but

Mrs Bendall was sitting there, waiting for her husband. When I expressed surprise that they hadn't returned to their hotel, I couldn't believe her response.

"If you go back before seven," she informed me. "You have to pay to get on the hotel car park."

For all his millions, Bendall was reluctant to put his hand in his pocket for what would surely have been no more than a pound to park his car. Given the chance, I would gladly have paid it, just to get rid of him.

The other chairmen during my time with the club have been more amenable. Harry Kartz was a Villa fanatic, who was always helpful to me. It was his encouragement, together with that of manager Ron Saunders, which persuaded me to apply for the secretary's job, and I will always be grateful for that. Then there was Sir William Dugdale, a real country gent who used to arrive for our home games in a battered old Morris Estate. He always wore *Plus Fours* and looked like he was ready for a day's shooting rather than a football match.

But none of them can claim to have had the same impact on the club's stature, or cared so passionately about Aston Villa, as Doug Ellis. True, he has his critics, anyone in his position is bound to offend someone somewhere along the line. But contrary to what some people may believe, he genuinely hates having to sack managers. During my time at the club, we have had nine managers, but every time Doug has had to dismiss anyone, it has bothered him deeply.

He certainly doesn't live up to his *Deadly* image in that respect, and for the record, I should point out that the nickname has nothing to do with his football activities. Away from the club, Doug's two main forms of relaxation are shooting and salmon fishing, and on one of his trips to the River Tay he was accompanied by Jimmy Greaves and a camera crew from Central TV, who were making a documentary about the chairman. Having displayed his skills by hooking a sizeable salmon, he displayed how the fish should be killed, by tapping it on the head. At which point Greaves came up with the nickname *"Deadly Doug"*.

I've travelled the world with Doug Ellis, and often watched in awe as he has proved such a fine ambassador, both for Aston Villa and for this country. Whenever he makes a speech, he always stresses that despite all the disharmony in the world, sport should bring people together.

While he invariably takes centre stage at official functions, however, he is always happy to indulge my enthusiasm for the music scene. During a pre-season trip to Germany in 1992, the team headed for Dresden after playing their first match against Bergmann Borsig – the club from which we had signed two young players, Matthias Breitkreutz and Stefan Beinlich – but the chairman and I stayed behind in Berlin to take in a bit of culture.

Having spent all day walking around the city, we decided to find somewhere to eat, and I suggested the Hard Rock Cafe. I'd previously visited the ones in London and Florida, and they were my idea of a great night out. I wasn't so sure the Hard Rock Cafe would be the chairman's cup of tea, so to get him interested, I explained how it was based on a music theme, suggesting that a similar establishment might be developed with a football concept.

It was a midweek evening, and I was relieved to see the Hard Rock Cafe was not too crowded, which might have put him off going inside. After being shown to our seats to the accompaniment of rock music from speakers scattered all over the building, a waitress came over. After ordering our food, Mr Ellis asked the waitress something which I didn't quite catch until she said "Pardon?" and he had to repeat it in a raised voice.

"Excuse me, my dear," he said. "Would you mind asking them to turn the music down?"

The waitress, an American girl, looked both surprised and amused by this request, but promised to see what could be done. I'm pleased to report that we dined to the background of throbbing rock sounds. Even the chairman doesn't always get his own way!

Chapter Thirteen

Uncle Eric

Of all the people I have known during a quarter of a century at Villa Park, one man stands out above them all. Eric Houghton's contribution to the club was incredible. He served them as a player, a manager, a director and ultimately as Senior Vice-President, an honour bestowed upon him in 1983.

For me, though, he was more than all of those things. Eric was like a second father or a favourite uncle. He took me under his wing almost from the moment I arrived at the club, and we remained close right to his death, just short of his 86th birthday, in May, 1996.

Eric's health had been failing for several years, and he had become rather forgetful. But you won't find anyone connected with Aston Villa who has anything but fond memories of a man who will always be a true Villa legend.

He may have made his mark as a lethal striker of a ball in his pre-War playing days, during which he scored 170 goals in 392 games for Villa; he may have led the club to FA Cup glory as manager of the 1957 team who beat Manchester United at Wembley. But most people around Villa Park will remember him far more for the courteous, gentlemanly manner in which he acted as elder statesman for the club in his later years.

He was regarded in such high esteem by everyone who knew him, and such was my respect for him that despite our enduring friendship, I never addressed him by anything other than Mister Houghton. Quite simply, he was a lovely, lovely man who didn't have a bad word to say against anyone. Except the Germans, that is. He hated the Germans with a passion.

This stemmed from a visit Villa made to Germany in May 1938, the year before the outbreak of World War II. During one of our countless long chats, Eric explained how the atmosphere was frosty between the opposing players, even though a further 16 months were to elapse before hostilities broke out between England and Germany.

Villa won the first match against a German Select XI 3-2 in Berlin, but it was the second game, in front of 70,000 in Stuttgart, which Eric always related to me in greater detail. Well, one particular incident at least.

With the score standing a 1-1, Villa were awarded a penalty. Eric, renowned for his fearsome shots from dead ball situations, duly placed the ball on the spot. As he did so, the German goalkeeper walked over to him and yelled: "You Eengleesh pig!" Whether this insult was an outburst of patriotism or merely a piece of gamesmanship, Eric never knew. Either way, he took great delight from unleashing an unstoppable shot for the winning goal, and giving a satisfied smile to the German 'keeper, who – he always insisted – ended up in the net with the ball! The last bit of the story was possibly a slight exaggeration, but Eric's telling of it was always compelling.

I first became aware of Eric's loathing of the Germans when he and I accompanied Villa's youth team to a tournament in Dusseldorf in April 1973. It was quite an honour for me to be chosen to represent the club on a trip abroad only 10 months after joining the club, but Mr Houghton and I had already become firm friends, barely a day passing when he didn't call into the offices to recount a few stories or offer me encouragement.

During that youth trip, he really opened up about his feelings towards our hosts, although they were never aware of his animosity. At the numerous functions we were required to attend, he was a model of good behaviour every time he rose to make a speech. But it's a good job our hosts couldn't hear some of the things he muttered underneath his breath! Another favourite Houghton story was one surrounding trips Villa used to make to Blackpool in the 1930s for a short break after the busy Christmas programme. As the players assembled at New Street Station, another of the club's finest goalscorers, Tom "Pongo" Waring, was invariably the only one without any luggage.

"Where's your suitcase?" his team-mates would ask, to which Waring would reply: "I've got everything I need in my pocket," producing a stiff, new collar which was intended as a replacement for the one he was wearing on the second day of the trip. Whenever Eric told me this story, I could never resist asking: "Is that why they called him Pongo?"

Unlike today's superstars, whose faces continually flash up on our television screens and in glossy magazines, the likes of Houghton and Waring were very much working class heroes and not always instantly recognisable when wearing their day-to-day clothes.

On one occasion when Villa were playing away to Birmingham City, Eric was given permission to travel to the ground independently because he was living in the area of the city beyond St Andrew's.

Having caught a tram from his home to the Outer Circle route, he had planned to hop on a bus to complete his journey to the Blues ground, only to discover such long queues that to wait would have resulted in him arriving late and being fined. Undeterred, Eric began walking the two miles to the ground, soon finding himself in the company of a Birmingham supporter who talked enthusiastically about that afternoon's eagerly-awaited Second City derby clash.

The two men exchanged views on the game, and Eric's friend even showed him a short cut through an allotment. Throughout the walk, there wasn't the slightest hint of recognition from the Blues supporter, the fellow simply didn't realise he was chatting to one of

Villa's star players. On arrival at St Andrew's, he said: "I'm going on the Spion Kop, how about you." Imagine the look on his face when Eric replied: "I'm going to the dressing room!" That was typical of Eric's dry sense of humour. He had enjoyed the company of the friendly Blues supporter, and was grateful for being shown a short cut which helped him to avoid being late. He certainly wasn't going to make an issue of the fact that he was a star footballer and the other guy was just a face on the terraces. I bet the Birmingham fan's pals refused to believe him when he told them he'd shown Eric Houghton of Aston Villa and England the quickest way to St Andrew's. Or maybe he thought better of admitting being of assistance to such a key figure from the enemy camp.

Eric could even find an appropriate quip for the most sombre of occasions. When he and I attended the funeral for Alan Instone, the former Birmingham City secretary, the church was packed to the rafters, which was hardly surprising. Alan had been a big help to me in my early years as Villa secretary, and like Eric, was one of those characters you couldn't help but like.

On the day of of the funeral, so many people wanted to pay their last respects that it was eventually standing room only. Mr Houghton, having observed the bulging congregation, turned to me and said: "They should have made it all-ticket, Steve!" This may sound a little disrespectful, but as with everything Eric ever said or did, it was meant with the best of intentions. I know Alan would have appreciated it, anyway.

Cheeky Alan Instone offers his congratulations after our League Championship success.

Chapter Fourteen

Lunch with Batman

It was the moment every father dreads. Arriving home from work one evening, I was greeted at the door by my wife Carolyn. She had something to tell me about our seven-year-old son Matthew, she said, and I wasn't going to be too pleased.

All sorts of things flashed through my mind. Had he been fighting in the playground? Been caught smoking behind the bikeshed? Played truant from his classes? It was none of these things. It was worse. Carolyn informed me that Matthew had taken a major decision – he had become a Newcastle United supporter.

The news that my son could even think about any other club than Villa came as a bolt out of the blue. I just wasn't ready for it. Like my own father, I had taken it for granted that my lad would, in his own time, declare himself a Villa supporter. What other choice is there after all, when your dad has been a lifelong supporter and is actually secretary of the club?

Instead, Matthew had pledged his allegiance to a club more than 200 miles away. Once I had recovered from the initial shock, I decided I needed someone to blame, and suddenly it dawned on me just how my son had been so misdirected in his choice of football club. It was that square box in the corner of the lounge.

Television, I reckon, has a lot to answer for. In my younger days, televised football was a rarity, so you went along to watch your local team on a Saturday afternoon, or sometimes a Wednesday evening, and read everything you needed to know about them in the local paper.

Not any more, you don't. Switch on the TV and you can watch live top-class football virtually every night of the week, without ever venturing beyond the front door. It is in this overkill environment that Matthew and thousands of other youngsters are growing up, and hardly surprisingly, they are heavily influenced by the opinions of those presenting the programmes. During the past few seasons, Newcastle United have been one of the most fashionable teams in the country, and if it hadn't been the Magpies, my boy could just have easily been drawn to the likes of Manchester United, Liverpool or Arsenal.

At least there was a positive side to Newcastle. When you support a team you invariably have a favourite player. Matthew opted for David Ginola – and suddenly became enthusiastic about the prospect of learning French. Initially, though, he was quite happy to be decked out in his black-and-white striped replica shirt, proudly bearing the name "Ginola".

He even met his new hero after we played the Geordies at Villa Park last season, my Newcastle counterpart Russell Cushing arranging for him to go into the visitors' dressing room and get the players autographs. Matthew told me later that Ginola had chatted to him (in English, I presume), but that Alan Shearer, Newcastle's £15m striker, had been soaking in the bath, and had not been able to sign his book.

That was rectified when we caught up with the England star before he left the ground, and I also managed to take a photograph, a copy of which is now on the wall of my office with the accompanying caption: *"£15m player – with Alan Shearer."*

Matthew, of course, was delighted to have met the world's most expensive footballer, but there was an even bigger treat to come a few weeks later. Villa's former Commercial Manager Tony Stephens, who looks after the business interests of Shearer, David Platt, Dwight Yorke and David Beckham, phoned to say he and Alan would be attending our game against Liverpool. He added that Alan would be happy to sign the photo I had taken, and was looking forward to meeting Matthew again. There were just two problems. The Liverpool game was a sell-out, and Matthew wasn't bothered about going anyway. For one thing, Newcastle weren't playing, for another, it was live on television.

When I explained this to Tony, he came up with a simple solution – he and Alan would call at our house on their way to Villa Park. Matthew was agog when I told him, and I just wish I could have been there to see his face when England's captain knocked at the front door. Unfortunately I couldn't be there because there was work to be done before the Liverpool match, including a guided tour for some City analysts in preparation for the club's Stock Market flotation. All the same, my mind was very much back at home as I showed them around, and even though it was only 15 minutes to kick-off when we finished, I couldn't resist phoning Carolyn to see how things had gone.

It had been brilliant, she informed me. Alan had stayed for 40 minutes, had a cup of tea, and chatted away to Matthew, without getting a great deal of response from the awestruck seven-year-old. By comparison, my younger son Jack had effectively run the show.

Informed that our visitor was a famous footballer, three-year-old Jack had produced his ball and asked Shearer to play with him. When he was told Alan couldn't do so because he had a poorly leg, Jack had disappeared for a few minutes before re-appearing with a bandage, which he promptly threw at the England star! Jack clearly believes actions speak louder than words. During his short life, he has already cut his own hair and needed hospital treatment to remove Bluetack which he had stuck up his nose. And having learned that his footballing guest was injured, he had headed straight for the First Aid kit to do something about it.

While Alan roared with laughter, I gather Matthew continued to sit quietly, not quite able to believe who had come to see him and sign his photograph. He was rather less subdued at school the following day, proudly announcing to anyone willing to listen that the great Alan Shearer had called round for tea. If he was looking to impress, however, he was bitterly disappointed. No-one believed him.

"Oh, yeah?" derided one of his mates. "And I had Batman round for lunch."

Chapter Fifteen

Just The Ticket

One thing worried me more than anything when I took over as secretary – the responsibility of handling a semi-final at Villa Park. I'd watched Alan Bennett do the job with apparent ease on numerous occasions, but with so much prestige involved in one of this country's showpiece football matches, it was an awesome prospect.

To make matters worse, Alan left the club on the day of the 1979 FA Cup semi-final. Arsenal beat Wolves 2-0, but my abiding memory is of a threatened strike by stewards, which could have thrown the occasion into chaos. Alan dealt with it in the most sensible manner – by agreeing to their demands for more money – and left me with the chilling words: "It's your problem from now on."

Had I realised what would be in store 12 months later, I might have resigned on the spot. The following Spring, we staged *three* semi-finals in the space of 16 days! Whenever the FA request your ground as a semi-final venue, they sometimes ask you to be on standby to host a replay from the other semi. So although West Ham beat Everton at Villa Park on Saturday, April 12, we suddenly found ourselves involved in arrangements for an Arsenal v Liverpool replay just four days later. And just to add to the headache, they drew 1-1, and returned to us on

Monday April 28. Even in the second replay, the Gunners and the Reds were unable to achieve a result, but thankfully we were spared a fourth semi-final, the teams finally settling their differences at Coventry City's Highfield Road.

It had been quite a baptism into the staging of semi-finals, although I was pretty well versed in the whole business by the time that third game rolled around. They always say that if you find something a worry, you should face it head on, although I didn't really have any choice in the matter. It was simply a case of getting on with it. Everything went pretty well according to plan, too, apart from one oversight on my part before the Everton v West Ham game. Quite simply, I overlooked the fact there would be two team coaches arriving at Villa Park – and there's only room for one outside the players' entrance.

The problem was solved by directing West Ham's coach to the main car park behind the North Stand, but unfortunately this didn't go down too well with Stan Taylor of S. W. Taylor, the club's insurance brokers. His car was blocked in and he was furious that he couldn't get away after the game. I didn't know Stan very well at the time, and he clearly didn't know me. I was just leaving the main reception door in a blue shirt and claret-and-blue club tie when he stormed across and demanded: "Can you shift your bloody coach?"

Totally unaware of what had happened, I merely replied: "Beg your pardon?", to which he snapped back: "You are the West Ham coach driver, aren't you?"

Even in his anger and frustration, Stan saw the funny side when he realised the mistake he had made, and to this day, whenever I phone him, I always say : "It's the West Ham coach driver here."

If the thought of organising a semi-final threw me into a cold sweat in those early days, at least that 1980 hat-trick gave me plenty of practice, and these occasions have always gone pretty much to plan in the intervening years.

One thing which has always helped is that FA Cup semi-finals are always all-ticket matches, which makes crowd control much more straightforward. It wasn't always like that for Villa matches, and I can recall numerous occasions when thousands of supporters have been locked out at cup ties or league matches which suddenly became high profile games.

In those days anyone turning up for big games ran the risk of going home disappointed (you might argue that those who got in were not always happy with what they saw, either), but I would like to think I played an important part in putting an end to lock-out situations at Villa Park.

The advent of all-seater stadiums has been a big help at grounds all over the country, of course, but even when we still had terracing at Villa Park, we had gone a long way to solving the problem of turning people away.

It used to annoy me when we had to turn people away, but a solution dawned on me one day when a guy called at the ground to buy seat tickets for a forthcoming match against Manchester United. When told that every seat had been sold, he asked how he could guarantee getting in, and the answer was simple – he couldn't.

The thought of this fellow being turned away from the turnstiles because the ground was full seemed totally unfair, particularly when he had been willing to buy seat tickets, so we took the step of making *every* Villa Park fixture all-ticket, both for seats and terracing.

The concept was that if we sold 30,000 tickets and had a 45,000 capacity, we knew we could accommodate a further 15,000 on the day of the match. If 18,000 happened to turn up, there was a ready-made answer for those who failed to get in. They should have bought tickets in advance. And whenever we approached a sell-out before match day, we took the precaution of advising supporters through the local media that only a limited number of places were available, and encouraged them to buy a ticket in order to avoid disappointment.

Even now the terraces have gone, this system still works effectively, which I'm sure is a big relief to the club and supporters alike. It's certainly a far cry from my early days at Villa. Although we were one of the first clubs to have an electronic counter, which told us exactly how many people had entered various areas of the ground, there was no way of controlling the numbers outside. On days when we were getting towards a capacity crowd there was only one way of gauging how many people were trying to get in. I used to ring our former Police Liaison Officer, George Brannigan, and he would lean out of the window to get an idea of the length of the queues. If they stretched beyond his line of vision, he would radio one of his men for the answer.

With the benefits of today's closed circuit television system, it now seems unbelievable that we had to rely on such basic methods. At least we have never had to worry about such matters at semi-finals, which have always been all-ticket games or, indeed, when Villa have been playing away in big matches. Sadly, there hasn't been the need to concern ourselves about the distribution of FA Cup Final tickets during my time at the club, but it's fair to say we have become well acquainted with the League Cup since its inception in 1960-61.

As a young supporter, I watched the home legs when Villa beat Rotherham in the inaugural Final and were beaten by the old enemy Birmingham City two years later, but it was only after the Final moved to Wembley in 1967 that the competition really took off. Before that, some of the bigger clubs had even declined to take part, but suddenly there was much more prestige about the League Cup.

Four years later we were back at the famous old stadium once again. By this time I was an employee of the club, and was able to savour my first taste of an Aston Villa banquet. There was plenty to celebrate, too. Ray Graydon's follow-up goal, after goalkeeper Kevin Keelan had saved his penalty, gave us a 1-0 victory over Norwich City. No expense was spared over the banquet, either. We gathered at London's Savoy Hotel for a slap-up meal, which was followed by cabaret from comedienne Joan Turner's sister. The lady's name escapes me, but she had us in stitches as she went through her comedy routine, especially when she decided to indulge in a spot of audience participation. Goalkeeper

Jimmy Cumbes drew the short straw, and ended up with our entertainer sat on his lap while she made fun of him. Like most goal-keepers, Jim's a big fellow, but when she started referring to his size, I don't think she was talking about his height. A lot of players would have died with embarrassment, even with a few glasses of champagne inside them, but Jimmy took it all in his stride.

It was quite a night, but even winning the League Cup doesn't guarantee a night's sleep at one of the world's top hotels. A shortage of bedrooms meant The Savoy were unable to accommodate everyone in the Villa party, so once the festivities were over, some of us had to make our way across the Strand to the Regent Palace Hotel.

The alternative sleeping arrangements, needless to say, did not detract from our euphoria. The same can hardly be said of the banquet which followed yet another Wembley appearance two years later. This time we avoided the bedroom problem by booking the Metropole Hotel on the site of the National Exhibition Centre, but other factors contrived to make it one of the biggest let-downs in the history of catering.

For starters, the 1977 final against Everton finished as a tedious goal-less draw, so there was hardly a reason for celebration when the issue was undecided. Even if we had lost, we could have spent the night drowning our sorrows, but the result left everyone with a feeling of anti-climax.

Plans to get the event under way at 9pm didn't exactly work out, either. The idea of returning to Birmingham was fine in theory, but anyone who has ever tried leaving Wembley in a hurry after a Cup Final will know what a nightmare the traffic can be. An hour or more after we were supposed to sit down to dinner, coaches were still arriving at the Metropole, and I don't think anyone had a great appetite. On top of that, all the staff were aware that we had to be up early the following morning in readiness for a 12-hour day selling tickets for the replay at Hillsborough.

If we thought the match at Sheffield would provide an outcome, we were mistaken. Once again, Villa and Everton drew – 1-1 this time – and in those days there was no penalty shoot-out to settle the matter. Once again, it was a case of getting down to the business of selling tickets for a second replay at Old Trafford, and even that match went to extra-time before Brian Little's second goal of the night gave us a 3-2 victory and the League Cup for the second time in three seasons.

When the club floated on the Stock Exchange, we had to produce a prospectus crammed with facts and figures about Aston Villa, and every line had to be verified before publication.

When we stated we were the sixth best supported club in the country, for example, we needed statistics to back up the claim. When we described our manager as a former popular player with the club, it had to be strictly correct, and not just someone's hasty judgement. Bearing in mind the immense respect Brian Little commanded among our fans during his playing days, I don't think anyone would dispute the accuracy of that Prospectus description. I can certainly produce a dozen members of Villa's staff, myself included, who would vouch for the authenticity of the statement. When Brian prodded the ball over the line at the Stretford End to settle the final saga, we could happily have invaded the pitch and mobbed him. Not only had he won the Cup, he had brought an end to what was the busiest and most concentrated period I have known at Villa Park.

The club even treated all the staff, plus their partners, to a short break in Torquay as a thank-you for all the effort which had been put in. Little could we have known, as we put our feet up for a couple of days and enjoyed the South Devon sunshine, that it would be 17 years before Villa would be involved in another League Cup Final. In the meantime, of course, there was the European Cup Final, but the number of tickets involved for the match in Rotterdam was nowhere near the volume you have to handle before a Wembley match.

By the time the 1994 final against Manchester United rolled around, there had been numerous changes of personnel behind the scenes at Villa Park, which meant it was a totally new situation for several members of staff, and even those of us who had been involved in the Everton marathon were rusty because it had been so long ago. Having said that, everything went reasonably smoothly. Unlike the FA Cup Final, where numbers are limited, each of the finalists receives plenty of tickets for a League Cup Final, which meant we were able to satisfy the demand of most of our regular supporters. The biggest headache in 1994, in fact, was over a single ticket required by the Lord Mayor of Birmingham for his son.

Because of his status, Paul Tilsley was invited to Wembley as the club's guest, which entitled him to a seat in the Royal Box, but when he asked about an extra ticket he was politely informed he would have to pay for that one. This didn't go down too well at the Council House, and Councillor Tilsley was clearly not in the best of moods when he phoned me to complain.

"Your office have been on to say I can have an extra ticket, but I have to pay for it," he said, in a tone which implied we should be offering him another complimentary seat.

"Yes, that's right," I informed him. "Even we have to pay for our family's tickets."

From here, the conversation went downhill fast, and I have to admit I lost my rag with the Lord Mayor. I don't make a habit of swearing, but I threw a couple of choice words into that heated telephone exchange. All the work involved in organising tickets had started to wear me down and I was furious that someone in his position should be asking for a free ticket when thousands of genuine fans were clamouring to pay for one. I may have been wrong to swear, but I certainly wasn't going to back down. The Lord Mayor eventually paid for his ticket, although the incident left a bitter taste. Even when I approached him during the pre-match lunch in the Wembley banqueting hall to apologise for my outburst, he was very short with me, insisting that the damage had been done, and claiming no-one had ever spoken to him like that.

Happily, his attitude did nothing to take the gloss off a marvellous weekend. While the team headed off to their country retreat hotel, the directors, myself and our wives travelled down to London on the Saturday for an overnight stay in a hotel and a meal organised by Doug Ellis. Not that I ended up dining with the chairman. For my wife Carolyn and myself, it was the rare chance of a night-out together because we had arranged for the children to be looked after, so we took a taxi instead to the West End for the stage production of *Grease*.

Later on, we met up with Nigel Kennedy and music promoter Tim Parsons at a Mexican restaurant our superstar fan had recommended. Typical of Nigel, who has no airs and graces despite his stardom, it was a dingy little place, little more than a small bar. I'd like to be able to say that the food compensated for the surroundings, but sadly it didn't. I struggled through a few mouthfuls of a strange-looking dish which almost sneered at you and dared you to try and get it past your lips, but Mrs Stride refused to eat a thing.

Equally unsavoury was the headline in one of the Sunday papers the following morning, proclaiming the alleged indiscretions of United chairman Martin Edwards. That was the last thing the Old Trafford club needed on the day they were playing in a Wembley final. But we had other things to occupy our minds. Even as our players were relaxing at their own hotel in readiness for the big match, we were involved in a meeting to organise more action for them in the form of an end-of-season tour to South Africa.

For the present, though, the only thing which mattered was beating United, and from the moment we set foot inside Wembley, you could sense it was going to be Villa's day. We may have been the underdogs, but while the Manchester fans were strangely subdued during the build-up, our supporters really got involved in the spirit of the occasion, transforming one half of the stadium into a sea of claret-and-blue and generating a wonderful carnival atmosphere.

The team were obviously in the right frame of mind, too. To put them at ease, manager Ron Atkinson had recruited Merseyside comedian Stan Boardman to entertain them on the coach, just as he had with Sheffield Wednesday three years earlier. Once again, it proved a master stroke, with Big Ron enjoying a laugh at the expense of the club who had sacked him. Wednesday had beaten United 1-0 in the 1991 League Cup Final, and Villa's 1994 triumph was an even more emphatic 3-1.

Our strikers Dalian Atkinson and Dean Saunders shared the goals, although the real hero was our Republic of Ireland international Paul McGrath, who played against his former club despite barely being able to lift his arm. The injury had been troubling Paul for some time and it was clear he might struggle to get through the whole game. But he was determined to play, and before the match, club doctor David Targett went down to the dressing room to give him a pain-killing injection. Doc asked me to go along with him, so I was able to lap up some of the pre-match atmosphere. I must confess, though, that I had to look away when Doc produced his syringe. Like a lot of other people, I get pretty squeamish when it comes to injections, even when I'm not on the receiving end of the dreaded needle.

Not that it detracted from my appetite when we sat down to a celebration dinner at the Royal Lancaster Hotel that night. Unlike the Metropole event 17 years earlier, there was no sense of anti-climax this time. I even had my own private cabaret. Seated with myself and Carolyn were my secretary Pam Silk and her husband Pete, Doug Ellis's personal assistant Marion Stringer and her husband Ted, plus two up-and-coming comedians who had just started presenting the *Fantasy Football* TV programme. Frank Skinner and David Baddiel had not really shot to prominence at the time, but they kept us amused right through dinner and long into the night.

At breakfast the next morning, we heard tales of people not even bothering going to bed, but toasting our success right through until daybreak. And who could blame them after such a long wait since our previous major honour? The whole weekend had gone off perfectly – or at least I thought it had until I got home later that day. Apart from the players, the Football League also give the finalists five other medals, one each for the manager, physio and secretary, plus another two for distribution at the club's discretion. These had been handed to me after the match, but in the euphoria of the occasion, I hadn't even bothered looking at them. It was only when a League official phoned in a state of panic that I realised we had been given the losers' medals. I know most people had expected United to win, but this was taking things too far!

Two years later we were back at Wembley, this time with Brian Little in charge, to take on Leeds United in the club's seventh League Cup Final. The team had become specialists in Coca-Cola Cup-ties, and it was getting to be good fun behind the scenes, too. If 1994 had involved shaking off the administrative cobwebs, 1996 was a breeze when it came to the business of organising a smooth ticket distribution operation.

You could tell the Football League were beginning to savour the big occasion, too. In the past, the only entertainment ahead of a League Cup Final was the traditional marching band, which was all very well in its own way, but didn't really cater for the young fan. Our match against Leeds, though, was preceded by a highly-entertaining programme of pop music and modern dance routines, culminating in a spectacular firework display as the teams emerged from the tunnel.

For millions of football supporters there's something magical about that tunnel, and it must be an exhilarating feeling to be a player or a manager taking those last few steps into daylight to be greeted by a mass of colour and a crescendo of noise. I have to say, though, that it doesn't have quite the same romantic feeling at the end of the match. Both team coaches are usually parked in there, ready to whisk the players away, and the dark and dingy tunnel invariably stinks of exhaust fumes.

The Wembley dressing rooms also leave a lot to be desired. They are neither very modern nor very large – the ones at Villa Park are at least half as big again – and it's total chaos in there at the end of a game. Not that anyone is too concerned about that if you have just won the

Cup, and my son Matthew certainly had no complaints when I took him down there following our 3-0 triumph over Leeds. He had his photograph taken both with the cup and with the players, and was able to join in the victory celebrations, which were ably led by our star striker Dwight Yorke.

Ever since he had joined us after our trip to his native Trinidad and Tobago in 1989, Dwight had matched his footballing talents with a bubbly personality, but the ***Calypso Kid*** was never more outgoing than during those Wembley festivities. He'd been left out against Manchester United two years earlier, and he was determined to make up this time.

Such was his popularity that during the build-up to the final, there had even been a cassette issued, a re-work of *New York, New York* under the title *It's Up To You Dwight Yorke*. It was never going to make the Top 20, but it soon became a popular new anthem on the Holte End. Our fans had been singing it, too, as the team went on their lap of honour at Wembley, and the tune had clearly stuck in Dwight's head. Having removed any inhibitions with a couple of gulps of champagne from the Cup, the boy from the Caribbean was ready to party. Standing stark naked in the middle of the room as his team-mates went through the process of getting changed, he suddenly began signing. "Start spreading the news, he's playing today..." He was no Frank Sinatra, but everyone present was only too happy to join in as the song picked up tempo.Every time the dressing room went quiet, Dwight would start again, even though the accompaniment was rather less enthusiastic when he launched into his sixth or seventh rendition!

Chapter Sixteen

Sign Of The Times

It's hard to believe that a team can actually celebrate losing a football match, but that was certainly the case when Aston Villa were beaten at Arsenal on the final day of the 1980-81 season.

Our 2-0 defeat was, in the final analysis, of absolutely no consequence. We had gone to Highbury requiring a draw to clinch the club's first League title for 71 years, but in the end even a share of the points wasn't needed. Ipswich Town, our closest rivals, lost at Middlesbrough that afternoon, and Aston Villa were crowned First Division champions.

Memories of the game have long since faded. I'm sure most of the 20,000 Villa fans who filled Highbury's old Clock End open terrace would struggle to offer much information about the proceedings, either. Many of them stood with their ears glued to transistor radios, more concerned about what was going on at Ayresome Park than the action unfolding before their eyes. Up in the Directors' Box, I attempted to look calm and composed. In reality my stomach was churning over the prospect of what we might achieve at the conclusion of that 90 minutes' football.

My recollections of the afternoon of May 2, 1981, are of meeting legendary Brazilian Pele, who was a guest of Arsenal for the day, of the

Gunners' assistant secretary David Miles continually dashing down to the Boardroom to bring us details of the Ipswich match, and of a phone call which put the finishing touch to a wonderful day. As I gazed across the sea of supporters celebrating our triumph on the pitch after the match, Arsenal secretary Ken Friar tapped me on the shoulder to say there was a call for me in his office.

Initially, I was just a bit annoyed at being dragged away from those marvellous scenes of jubilation, but my mood changed as I picked up the receiver. On the other end of the line was Alan Instone – secretary of Villa's deadliest rivals Birmingham City.

"You know how much I hate the Villa," he said. "But I felt I had to ring and say *well done*." The gesture was typical of Alan, a man with whom I'd developed a close relationship, even though we were secretaries of the Second City's footballing rivals. It wasn't just a question of me working for Aston Villa and Alan for Birmingham City, either. We were not just secretaries of the respective clubs, we were also staunch supporters. And like the fans who frequent Villa Park and St Andrew's, he had no time for Villa and I had no time for Blues.

But that didn't stop us from becoming the best of friends, and I'll always be grateful for the help and encouragement he gave me after I had been appointed secretary of Villa in 1979. I was only 28 at the time, and very much a novice. By comparison, my counterparts at the other West Midland clubs were all well-established and respected. There was Alan Everiss at West Bromwich Albion, Phil Shaw at Wolves and Alan at Birmingham.

These guys had been doing the job for years, and although there was no doubt in my mind that Villa were the top club in the area, it was a daunting prospect trying to match the efficiency which they had perfected through experience. Alan, though, was always ready to offer a helping hand whenever I needed it, and many of our dealings were conducted in the most pleasant of environments – the pub. We lived just around the corner from each other in the Hodge Hill district, and if ever we had any documents to exchange, the business was invariably conducted over a pint at an establishment called "The Hunter's Moon".

Before long, the "Moon" became a regular rendezvous for Alan and myself at the end of the working week. We would meet around 6pm on a Friday, and knock back three or four pints during the next hour or so. It wasn't only as a club secretary that Alan was more experienced than me. He was a seasoned drinker, and when we left the pub, you would never have guessed a drop of alcohol had passed his lips. Not me. I never got drunk as such, but more often than not I would fall asleep as soon as I got home and settled down in front of the television. But I used to look forward to an hour relaxing with the man from the Blues, and engaging in a bit of light-hearted banter with the "enemy". I'm sure Alan enjoyed those sessions, too. He really liked his pint, but he also enjoyed company, particularly when the conversation automatically turned to football.

On the final day of that 1980-81 season, Blues were playing Everton at home, and like everyone else at St Andrew's, I've no doubt that Alan was secretly hoping Villa would be pipped at the post for the title. Once the news had filtered through that we were Champions, however, he was straight on the phone with his message of congratulations. He would have been biting his lip at the time, but I know he would have been personally delighted for his Friday evening drinking partner.

Alan would also have acknowledged what an outstanding feat Aston Villa achieved that season. Not only did we win the Championship, we did it by using just 14 players all season, and not one of them cost a fortune. Peter Withe had become the club's record signing when he joined us from Newcastle United for £500,000 the previous summer, but even in those days that wasn't an enormous fee, the £1m barrier already having been broken.

What I'm trying to say is that money doesn't always guarantee success, and that has been particularly true in Aston Villa's case. Nearly a decade elapsed before we surpassed the Withe fee by paying £650,000 for Bradford City striker Ian Ormondroyd, and it's fair to say that our subsequent record signings, with the exception of Dean Saunders, have all found their price tags a heavy burden. Neither Tony Cascarino nor Dalian Atkinson were huge successes, and more recently Sasa Curcic has found difficulty in justifying his transfer fee.

Yet lower down the scale our managers have unearthed some priceless gems down the years. Graham Taylor always claimed he paid over the odds when David Platt joined us from Crewe for £200,000, yet we ultimately made the biggest transfer profit in the club's history when Platt jetted off to Italy to join Bari for £5.5m. Dwight Yorke cost us just £10,000 when he gave up his sunshine life in the Caribbean in 1989, now his value is nearer £10m. By modern day standards, the likes of Ian Taylor, Alan Wright, Gary Charles and Ugo Ehiogu have been modest purchases, but each has played an important part in the club's success over the past couple of years.

Regardless of the fee, though, you have to adhere to rigid regulations when signing a footballer. The deadline for signings used to be 5pm on a Thursday afternoon, then it switched to mid-day on Friday, and managers have a perennial habit of cutting things fine. I'm willing to bet that if you could sign a player up to 2pm on match day, someone would be wheeled in at lunchtime.

These days, thankfully, the business of getting players registered in time is aided by modern technology. The advent of the fax machine means that everything can be done and dusted in a matter of minutes once all the transfer forms have been signed. But it wasn't always like that.

When the Thursday afternoon deadline was in force and a deal was being rushed through at the last minute, we had to send a telegram to the Football League headquarters, stating that the forms relating to the transfer had been posted before 5pm. Then we just had to hope the forms would get from Witton Post Office to Lytham St Anne's by Saturday morning – and would be found to be in order. Any mistakes, and we knew there would be a phone call informing us we couldn't field our new player.

You wouldn't believe how closely the forms were scrutinised. Luckily, the only time I made an error happened to be when we signed someone during a close season. The forms were duly posted – and four days later they were back on my desk. The reason for their return was that the player's signing-on fee was £10,000, payable in three annual instalments. Our forms stated that he would receive three payments of £3,333.33p, but our arithmetic wasn't accurate enough for the League. They sent me a letter explaining that the final payment should actually be £3,333.34p! We were able to laugh it off, but had the transfer taken place during the season, it would have meant a debut being delayed for the sake of a penny.

There were times, of course, when we couldn't even rely on the nation's postal and telegram systems. When we signed Dennis Mortimer from Coventry City in December 1975, I had to drive up to Lytham on Christmas Eve. Our manager Ron Saunders had agreed the deal the previous night, and wanted Mortimer to make his debut against West Ham on Boxing Day. The forms obviously weren't going to get to the League by post, so there was only one thing for it. I had to deliver them by hand – and it meant an early start, too, because the League's offices were closing at mid-day for the festive season. Luckily, everything went through in time and a crowd of over 51,000 enjoyed Mortimer's first match for Villa, a 4-1 win against West Ham.

Another transfer which stands out in my memory is that of Andy Gray to our Midland neighbours Wolves, not long after I had taken over as secretary. There's always far less work involved when you are selling, both in terms of negotiating with the player and filling in forms, but the Gray transfer was notable because it created a British record, a reported £1,469,000.

Even with such a huge amount of money involved, however, our chairman Ron Bendall was as matter-of-fact about the transaction as he might have been about selling a second-hand car. Once the fee had been agreed, he simply told me to get over to Wolverhampton and get on with it.

All told, I must have handled over £100 million worth of transfers, in and out, since 1979, although numerous deals have gone through while I've been on holiday. That trend was set with the arrival of Tony Morley from Burnley in the summer following my appointment, and more recently I've returned from sunning myself on foreign shores to discover we have signed the likes of Gareth Southgate, Savo Milosevic and Fernando Nelson.

But one Villa signing landed me what most people would describe as the trip of a lifetime, even though it ultimately resulted in Villa being fined by the Football Association for making illegal payments to an agent.

No transfer fee was involved when we signed goalkeeper Mark Bosnich from Australian club Sydney Croatia, but the deal was the most complicated I have known. Bosnich had previously played a couple of times for Manchester United, but had been forced to return home because he did not qualify for a work permit.

That might well have been the end of his career in this country, but our interest was aroused when Graham Smith, a former West Brom goalkeeper and now a football agent, approached manager Ron Atkinson to say Bosnich's father had bought his release from his Australian club.

Ron's interest may have gone no further, but our chief scout Brian Whitehouse knew Bosnich from his days at Old Trafford, and suggested it might be something worth pursuing. Bozzie eventually joined us in February 1992, but I was despatched *Down Under* two months before that to lay the groundwork.

When people go to Australia, it's usually for two or three weeks, but in my case it was a whirlwind trip involving six days and five nights. Britain was both ice-bound and fog-bound when Graham Smith and I flew out from Heathrow, but after a 17-hour flight I celebrated my 41st birthday on Perth beach in temperatures which soared into the nineties.

After two nights there, we flew on to Sydney for a couple of days, during which I established from Bosnich's father, Mark senior, that he had, indeed, purchased his son's registration from Sydney Croatia, which meant he was free to join a club in England.

Manchester United weren't too happy when they learned we had pinched Bozzie from under their noses, insisting they had an understanding he would return to Old Trafford if ever he came back to this country, but we did everything by the book. Well, almost everything. Where we stepped out of line slightly was by paying Graham Smith for setting the deal up, and we were subsequently ordered to pay a £35,000 fine for making illegal payments to an agent.

These days, dealing with an agent is acceptable, as long as he is licensed, but even before the procedure was authorised, it was an open secret that these guys played a substantial role in transfer activity. I frequently sat in on salary negotiations where a player would ask to be excused for 10 minutes to think something over. What he really meant was that he wanted to nip down to the car park to consult his adviser.

At least everything is out in the open under the new regulations, although conducting negotiations with agents can be both tedious and frustrating. They obviously want to get the best possible deal for their client (particularly if it means a bigger commission going into their own pockets), but some advisers are pernickety beyond belief.

I won't embarrass the fellow concerned by naming him, but one agent really made my blood boil after we had agreed a multi-million pound contract for the player he was representing. One of the stipulations of a footballer's contract is that you have to state a weekly salary, so having divided the annual figure by 52, I simplified things by knocking off the pence.

I couldn't believe it when the manager told me the agent wanted a word because a mistake had been made. I was even more staggered that the gentleman in question had calculated that over the duration of the contract, the pennies which had been omitted would have amounted to £124. I told him that if he was honestly bothered about his client missing out on less than £1-a-week after negotiating such a huge contract, he was pathetic. After a moment's thought, he seemed to agree. The contract forms remained unaltered.

It's not always agents who cause you problems, though. Dealing with clubs in other countries can also be quite a headache at times. When David Platt went to Bari, a sell-on clause was agreed, entitling Villa to a percentage of any profit if Platt was subsequently transferred for more than £5.5m. A year later, when he joined Juventus in a reported £6.5m deal, we naturally expected our cut. But the Italians manufactured the transaction in such a complicated way, with player exchanges and conflicting valuations, that they claimed there had been no profit. All we ever got was a warning to Doug Ellis not to pursue the matter – and when such threats emanate from that part of the world, you tend not to contradict them.

There were also financial irregularities when Dalian Atkinson joined Turkish club Fenerbahce in the summer of 1995. The transfer fee was 650,000 dollars, payable in instalments, but the payments suddenly stopped after we had received only 250,000 dollars. Atkinson had found life in the Asian sector of Istanbul quite a culture shock, not least the gruesome ritual when a sheep was slaughtered on the pitch and he was required to dab the animal's blood on his forehead.

After a reasonable start, he had lost his place in the team, at which point Fenerbahce took it upon themselves to cancel the cash drafts they had been sending us. Although we took up the matter with the Football Association, months dragged by while we waited for the remaining 400,000 dollars. Only when FIFA, the sport's world governing body, set a deadline for payment did Fenerbahce condescend to cough up the money they owed. Even then, they left it until the very last day before settling the balance. Turks may be full of Eastern promise, but getting them to keep it is quite another matter.

Chapter Seventeen

Day Trippers

Even super-fit professional footballers are not immune when those dreaded flu bugs start doing the rounds. Anyone who has been confined to bed with influenza for a few days will appreciate that no amount of treatment is going to make you feel any better. Every winter we hear that one club or another has been hit by a flu epidemic, leaving the manager waiting anxiously to conduct a Saturday morning roll-call which will determine how many fit players he has available for that day's game.

Such problems, unfortunately, are not confined to days of sub-zero temperatures. One of the biggest panics Aston Villa experienced was on a beautifully warm weekend in April 1988, less than 24 hours before we were due to play Crystal Palace at Selhurst Park.

We were chasing promotion from the old Second Division at the time, and with only a few games to go, manager Graham Taylor was desperate to field his strongest possible team for what is always a difficult away fixture.

Graham and the players travelled south on the Friday to stay at a hotel on the outskirts of London and get a good night's rest before a crucial game, but it didn't quite turn out that way. On the Friday evening, Graham phoned me at home to say several of the players had developed flu symptoms. Although he was hopeful everyone would be okay, he asked me to take winger Tony Daley down with me the following day, just in case he was needed.

Most football supporters living north of Watford Gap will agree that Palace is the worst away trip in the country. From the Midlands, the likes of Newcastle and Sunderland may be a lot further, but they are infinitely more straightforward. Reaching Selhurst Park involves a trip down the M40, a massive sweep around the M25, and then a tedious crawl through Croydon and into South London, where the traffic seems to get heavier with every mile.

It's a journey I've made on countless occasions, but I invariably end up tired and irritable by the time I reach Thornton Heath, where Selhurst Park is located. With this in mind, and the fact that Graham liked to get his players to an away ground no later than 2pm, I picked up Tony at 10am, leaving four hours for the journey. It should have been plenty of time, and probably would have been, even allowing for an accident which brought the London Orbital to a standstill.

The trouble was, I got lost – and the cosmopolitan community of South London are not the most knowledgeable when it comes to the location of Crystal Palace FC. Every time we stopped to ask for directions, we either received blank looks, or rather less than helpful replies like "Dunno, mate, it ain't round 'ere."

To make matters worse, the more we panicked, the heavier the traffic became. It occurred to both myself and Tony that we might not even get to the ground by kick-off time, which wasn't going to make either of us very popular with a manager preparing a flu-hit squad for a vital promotion battle. By the time we arrived it was 2.45pm, 15 minutes after the team sheet had to be handed in. It was too late for Daley to be included in the squad, even if Graham needed him.

Much to our relief, that wasn't the case. The lads who had felt unwell had recovered and the manager was able to field the team he had named the previous day. We managed a 1-1 draw, too, David Platt's goal earning us a point which ultimately helped us to finish runners-up to

Millwall. But what I couldn't quite understand at the time was why Graham didn't seem too angry over Tony's late arrival. After all, the lad might well have been needed, and I certainly felt I had let the club down badly. Instead of giving me a ticking-off for not allowing sufficient time, though, Graham merely shrugged and said: "Don't worry, Steve, no problem."

It was only after the match that I discovered why he had been so understanding. The team coach had also been held up in traffic and had arrived barely a quarter of an hour before us, which meant the club had only narrowly avoided a fine for handing in the team sheet late. So much for the wisdom of travelling overnight!

To be fair, the policy of teams travelling on the day before a match usually makes a lot of sense, and has become more and more commonplace over the last few years. It also means that myself, the chairman and the club's other directors no longer accompany the players to away matches, as we did a few years ago. I must confess it's something I occasionally miss, and it was certainly quite a thrill to be on the team bus as it edged through crowds of supporters in Rotterdam before the 1982 European Cup Final.

But with overnight stays now the norm rather than the exception, it's hard to justify leaving Villa Park on a Friday lunchtime and not getting home until late on a Saturday night. Quite apart from half a day's work being left behind, Caroyln and the kids would not exactly be impressed at the thought of me being away every other weekend.

In more recent times, Doug Ellis, myself and the club's two doctors David Targett and Barrie Smith have met on the morning of the game at the chairman's house, and I've driven us to the opposition ground, usually in time for lunch with our counterparts at the home club. Sometimes, though, it's a wonder this particular branch of the Aston Villa Travel Club ever got to a game on time.

It doesn't help that the chairman is unquestionably the worst passenger I have ever driven. You can bet we have hardly pulled off his drive when he states the obvious. If we're going to Arsenal he will ask if I'm going on the M1, if it's Manchester United he will suggest the M6. And I'm sure he only says these things because he knows how much it irritates me.

Once the route has been established, Mr Ellis really comes into his own as a back-seat driver. Whichever lane we happen to be in, he will suggest we could be going a bit faster in another one. To pacify him, I tend to move across – invariably to find he has changed his mind. The number of times we have zig-zagged up and down Britain's motorway system, I'm amazed I haven't been pulled over by the police and breathalysed. But at least Saturday mornings are nice and relaxed. It's still officially a working day, of course, but like any football supporter, we are all eagerly looking forward to the game, discussing Villa's prospects and what team the manager will select.

Most journeys to away grounds are pretty straightforward, although in some cases the last couple of miles can be a bit tricky. This is where Barrie Smith takes over. Or, at least, he's supposed to. I've lost count of the times I've reached a junction, and been uncertain which way to turn. "Okay, Barrie, which way now?" is the usual request. I may as well be asking for a prescription for backache as the good doctor ponders his reply. Invariably, I end up making the decision myself. Equally invariably, I get it wrong, particularly when we're on our way to Selhurst Park.

Thankfully, we usually allow ourselves plenty of time for away trips, so there's never much danger of being late, and I'm proud to relate that in 18 years as club secretary, I've only missed three competitive Villa games. One of those was the second leg of a Coca-Cola Cup-tie at Wigan, when I was in Turkey, sorting out arrangements for our UEFA Cup tie against Trabzonspor. As we were 5-0 up from the home leg, I didn't lose a great deal of sleep over having to give the return game a miss.

I would, however, have been bitterly disappointed had my absences risen to four when we reached the 1996 FA Cup semi-final. And at one stage it looked a distinct possibility. The problem wasn't ill health, but the fact that on the afternoon Villa were playing their first FA Cup semi-final for 36 years, we were staging the other semi-final.

While I desperately wanted to be at Old Trafford for our game against Liverpool, there was no way I could go AWOL from my duties at Villa Park, where Manchester United were playing Chelsea. Or could I? Suddenly, it dawned on me that once the match at Villa Park was under way at 1pm, my presence wasn't really necessary – and Villa's game didn't kick-off until three hours later.

Bearing in mind the likely traffic congestion on the M6, there was little point in attempting to journey by road, so I suggested to Doug Ellis that we could fly to Manchester. As soon as the referee's whistle had blown to get the United-Chelsea match under way, we jumped in the car and drove four miles to Sandwell Park Golf Club, where we were whisked into the sky by a helicopter the chairman had hired. Half an hour later, we landed at a small airport in Cheshire, and a taxi was waiting to speed us to the ground.

I wish I could say the effort was all worthwhile. Unfortunately, it wasn't. The afternoon ended in anti-climax. Our lads had performed superbly at Wembley seven days earlier to beat Leeds United 3-0 in the Coca-Cola Cup Final, but they never got going against Liverpool. We lost by the same margin, and that defeat ranks among my biggest disappointments in football. After nearly four decades as a Villa supporter, I still hadn't seen my team reach Wembley in an FA Cup Final.

That wasn't the only time I've taken to the skies for a Villa match in this country. The whole squad, plus a fair number of fans, travelled by plane to Norwich for our Premiership game at Carrow Road on New Year's Day, 1992. We lost that match, too, so perhaps we should keep our feet firmly on the ground for all future domestic excursions.

Travelling away, to be honest, will never be the same again. On the final away-day of the 1996-97 campaign, David Targett watched Villa in action for the last time. We returned later than usual that night, having stopped for a meal on the long trek from Middlesbrough, and it was around 11pm when I dropped off my three passengers at the chairman's house. Despite our 3-2 defeat, "Doc" had been in good spirits during the trip, but he realised as soon as he got home that something was seriously wrong. Our medical man diagnosed his own brain haemorrhage and immediately asked his wife to get him to hospital. He died two weeks later.

I've lost some close friends down the years, but Doc was the closest of all. He'd been the club's medical officer for over 25 years and we'd got along famously from the time I met him. He was even best man at my wedding, and we shared some great times on club trips abroad. He was a Villa man through and through, and like any other supporter, his mood on homeward journeys was invariably dictated by how the team had performed.

It always seemed a long way back to Birmingham if Villa had lost, and you wouldn't find a great deal of lively conversation from Messrs Ellis, Targett, Smith and Stride.

A win, though, put a totally different complexion on the situation. For the first half an hour or so, we would all be in buoyant mood, reliving every aspect of the match and giving marks out of 10 for all the Villa players, although I was usually the only one awake for the remainder of the trip. After a win, you see, the chairman and the two doctors were not averse to a drop of Scotch with our hosts, and they all tended to nod off once the monotony of motorway travelling took its hypnotic hold. If the combination of the drink and the drone of the engine didn't send my passengers to sleep, it was time to revert to Plan B. David Mellor's *6.06* radio programme usually did the trick.

Chapter Eighteen

That Floating Feeling

"I'll tell you what lads," said the Cockney cabbie as his taxi crawled through the notorious London traffic congestion. "I really feel sorry for Glenn Hoddle. He doesn't really pick the England team, you know. It's those old farts on the International Committee." When fits of laughter burst forth from the back seat, the driver must have thought he had landed himself a king-size tip. What he didn't know, and we did, was that one of those *old farts* would be paying his fare.

The countdown to Villa's flotation on the London Stock Exchange was a pretty serious business, but it also had its lighter moments. Like that day in the taxi when the chairman of Aston Villa, who just happened to be a member of the FA's International Committee, went unrecognised by the driver taking him to his next appointment. Had the cabbie realised after his dig at the England set-up that one of his passengers was Doug Ellis, I'm sure he would have died with embarrassment. Instead, he must have been totally bemused when myself, Mr Ellis and our newly-appointed director Mark Ansell fell about laughing.

Mark, together with solicitor David Owen, had been appointed to the Board a couple of weeks earlier, after we had been given the go-ahead at an Extraordinary General Meeting to become Aston Villa plc.

The question of going public had been brought up by shareholders at the club's annual meeting the previous August, and at that stage the answer had been no, we didn't intend to go down that particular road. As the season progressed, however, and other clubs floated on the stock market, we decided the time was right to become a public limited company. Football has long been acknowledged as big business, and a new share issue seemed the perfect way of generating funds to stay abreast of the Premiership's elite.

It certainly meant quite a windfall for Villa's existing shareholders, many of whom had bailed the club out of financial difficulties by buying shares in 1969 for £5. Over the years, those shares had soared in value to over £1,500, which must rank as one of the best investments a football supporter could ever make. I heard one story of someone who had been left a *special* share, which originally cost £75, in his father's will. At the time of the flotation, its value was roughly £18,000.

But it wasn't just a question of going public and taking the money. This was a different league for us. We spent week after week burning the candle at both ends to ensure that everything was in order and that every Stock Exchange regulation was adhered to, right down to the finest detail. One of the requirements was that a deputation from Villa embarked on a "roadshow" to generate interest in the flotation among the country's major financial houses, which is how the chairman, Mark and myself came to discuss Glenn Hoddle's selection powers with a London taxi driver.

That wasn't the only down-to-earth moment during a whistle-stop tour in which our feet never seemed to touch the ground. In a matter of 11 days, we gave nearly 50 presentations to a total of around 80 institutions, ranging from banks to insurance companies. Our road-show started on a Monday morning with a flight to Edinburgh, continued in Glasgow the following day and then moved to the City of London. Throughout that hectic week-and-a-half, the routine followed a similar pattern of two or three presentations to fund managers in the morning, a bigger session for larger groups from different companies over lunch, and then back to individual meetings throughout the afternoon.

The idea of standing in front of financial experts and giving a speech was just a little nerve-racking at first, but by the time we had given 30 "performances", it all became very straightforward – almost boring, to be honest. After the chairman had given his opening gambit about the football industry in general and Villa in particular, I followed up with a brief history of the club and our achievements, plus details of our ground and facilities before Mark outlined the financial picture. This was all very straightforward – until Mr Ellis started pinching some of my lines. Like an actor, I had a script to deliver, but on more than one occasion, the chairman allowed himself to get carried away with his introduction. In numerous instances I had to give him a thunderous glare to make him realise that he was stealing my glory.

In between each presentation, it was a case of climbing in and out of taxis, and trying to negotiate the heavy traffic which makes our capital city such a nightmare for commuters. On the Wednesday evening, however, the team were playing Wimbledon at Selhurst Park, which gave us a good excuse to take a break. Once the day's business was completed at around 5pm, we decided the most sensible route to South London was by rail rather than road. This proved to be a wise choice, particularly in view of previous experiences in trying to reach Selhurst in the car.

Even allowing for stops at various stations along the way, the train journey from central London to Thornton Heath took barely 20 minutes, where it would have been an hour or more by road. It was certainly unusual for the chairman to be travelling with commuters, but he seemed to enjoy the hustle and bustle as football fans mingled with office workers returning home from the City. We even popped into a pub in Thornton Heath before the match before joining supporters in a brisk walk up the High Street to the ground. After all the chasing around of the previous few days, it was nice to just sit back and enjoy a football match, particularly as Villa scored a 2-0 win over a Wimbledon outfit who have always been regarded as our bogy team.

But the game against the Dons was a brief respite. The following morning it was back to the roadshow, which rolled into the following week as we went through the routine of presentations, taxi rides and working lunches. Just how entertaining our efforts were, I don't know, but we weren't there to get laughs, just to create interest in the club's flotation.

The final performances of this whistle-stop tour were delivered on the Thursday of the second week, otherwise known as *Impact Day*. First we addressed around 30 members of the media in order to achieve maximum publicity, and this was followed by a final show for a gathering of fund managers. We achieved a sell-out situation, too, with the institutions going for our share issue in a big, big way. It was three times over-subscribed.

No doubt the money men were more impressed with the potential of our shares than the manner in which we sold the club at those presentations. Either way, that's what I call winning over your audience.

Chapter Nineteen

A Week In The Life

MONDAY, 27 JANUARY

So you thought a secretary's working day started at 9am? Not today, it doesn't. I've been summoned by the Crown Prosecution to give evidence at the football bribery trial at Winchester Crown Court, and been instructed to be there by 9.45. Bruce Grobbelaar, Hans Segers and John Fashanu stand accused of fixing matches, and as Fashanu is a former Aston Villa player, the prosecution want me to present details of his contract, signing-on fee and banking arrangements during his time with us.

Carolyn makes sure I'm out of bed by 5.30am, and an hour later, after a slice of toast, a cup of tea, a shower and a shave, I'm on the road. This is strange territory for me, and I'm surprised just how busy the M40 is at such an early hour. Still, it's not a bad run until I hit the infamous Newbury traffic jam, which makes me relieved I gave myself extra time for the journey.

On arrival at Winchester I'm greeted by a lady from an organisation called Witness Support, a group of volunteers who offer guidance to people who have never attended a court hearing. She shows me around the courtroom, explaining that the judge will be seated on the left and the defendants on the right, with the witness box in the middle. This, my new friend informs me, is where the Rose West murder trial took place a few months earlier, which cheers me up no end.

Then we move through to the witness room, where I'm pleased to see a couple of my football counterparts, Southampton secretary Brian Truscott and Wimbledon chief executive Dave Barnard, who are also there to give evidence. After a few minutes, however, my Witness Support chum pops her head round the door to say she showed me the wrong courtroom, and would I come and take a look at the one they would actually be using? This is fine, except that it is effectively a mirror image of the first room, with the judge's seat on the right and the dock on the left. I'll have to make sure I don't forget which way we're kicking.

On the way back to the witness room, we bump into Fashanu, dressed as slickly as he always is and flashing the sort of wide smile which delighted audiences when he hosted television's *Gladiators* programme. Fash really is a charming guy, and greets me with a big hug. "Steve, how are you?" he asks. "Great to see you again."

The Witness Support lady, alarmed at such a friendly gesture between the accused and a witness, tells me: "I don't think you're supposed to do things like that. But isn't he lovely!"

Back in the witness room, myself, Brian Truscott and Dave Barnard have been joined by three other people, and I detect a strange accent from one of the guys. It turns out he has flown over from Zimbabwe to give evidence against Grobbelaar, and it's clear that he doesn't fancy it one bit. We're all given the statements we made earlier (in my case, more than a year ago), to refresh our memories, and Dave is told he will be first to take the stand.

While Dave is away, our visitor from Zimbabwe is requested to leave the room, and when he returns five minutes later, his nervous expression has been replaced by a huge grin. "Would you believe it?" he says, "They don't need me after all." He hasn't been told the reason, but why should he care? Suddenly, a daunting prospect has turned into a short holiday in a foreign country, courtesy of the British taxpayer.

His happy departure from the scene means a change in the running order, and I'm next in. It's a nerve-racking business, giving evidence. I'm probably there no more than five minutes, but it seems more like an hour as I dutifully but nervously reiterate the information I had given in my original statement. One extra question is thrown at me – was Fashanu popular at the club? I can only tell the truth. Although his spell at Villa Park was hardly a success, and was blighted by the injury which prompted his retirement from football, Fash's beaming personality had made him immensely popular with players and staff alike.

Throughout my time in the witness box, I deliberately avoid meeting the glance of the defendants. But walking out, I look up to where they are sitting. There's Fash, with another massive grin on his face, putting his thumbs up. He obviously feels my evidence has been more beneficial to him than to the prosecution.

With the help of another hold-up in Newbury, it's around 4pm by the time I get back to Villa Park, and I spend the next hour and a quarter going through the day's correspondence with my secretary Pam Silk. Just before leaving the ground, I give Brian Truscott a ring to see how he got on. It turns out a recess had been taken for lunch just before he was due to appear, and his request to go to the pub had been frowned upon. Rather than offend the British judicial system, he had gone to a hotel for a drink instead! On his return, would you believe it, he had been told he wasn't needed after all. Some people have all the luck.

We have a Pontin's Central League fixture that evening, so after something to eat and half an hour with the family, I head off to Walsall's Bescot Stadium, where our reserve matches are being played. The game against Preston ends goalless, but during the evening I have a chat with a few former Villa people. John Ward, our assistant manager during Graham Taylor's reign, is there in his capacity as Burnley's No 2, while another of Taylor's former right-hand men, Steve Harrison, is now working for Preston.

Swindon Town manager Steve McMahon, who played for Villa in the 1980s, is also at Bescot, and tells me he is keen to take full-back Phil King on loan. As we are talking, Phil collapses in a heap, and is carried off with a pulled hamstring. Signing players can be a hazardous business.

TUESDAY, 28 JANUARY

We get word that the club's proposed Stock Market flotation, a topic which has been the subject of media speculation for some considerable time, is to go ahead. As a legal requirement, I have to arrange for a letter to go to all our players and staff, informing them of this development, although it is stressed that the story must be kept under wraps until an official announcement is made on February 2.

Among my telephone conversations this morning are one with Wimbledon's Dave Barnard to exchange notes on how we fared in the witness box at Winchester yesterday, and another with Coventry City secretary Graham Hover to make arrangements for the re-staging of our Premiership fixture at home to the Sky Blues. The game is scheduled for Saturday February 15, but Coventry will have to travel to Blackburn for a fourth round FA Cup-tie that day if they win their third round replay away to non-League Woking.

Manager Brian Little calls into my office at lunchtime, to discuss the details of a new contract for our young Republic of Ireland midfielder Gareth Farrelly and the restructuring of the club's youth scheme. Aware of the importance of nurturing home-grown talent, Brian proposes to bring in a couple of new members of staff to assist Brian Jones, our Youth Development Officer.

Of all the managers I have known in my time as secretary, Brian is undoubtedly the most open. He calls in at Villa Park every day after training at Bodymoor Heath, and I always feel relaxed in his company. He is willing to listen to your opinion, even though he won't necessarily be swayed by it.

Later, there's a call from Roy Hattersley's office. Although he is the Labour MP for the Sparkbrook district of Birmingham, Hattersley's footballing allegiance lies with Sheffield Wednesday, and he wants a ticket for our home match against the Owls tomorrow. There's a growing trend of politicians watching football these days, with Kenneth Clarke a regular at Nottingham Forest, Tony Blair at Liverpool and David Mellor at Chelsea. John Major is also a keen Chelsea fan, and I've met him on a couple of occasions, once at Stamford Bridge and also when we played Arsenal at Highbury. I have a feeling he has a sneaking regard for Aston Villa. When I asked for his autograph, he wrote: "Steve, best wishes, John Major – my father was a Villa supporter."

With such sound parental guidance, I wonder how Mr Major went astray when it came to choosing his favourite team?

Wednesday, 29 January

Match day. I must have been involved in over 500 of these, and down the years they have become second nature. But there's still a special buzz around the place when you know the team are due to play, whether it's a Saturday afternoon match or a midweek evening game.

My day starts around 9am, and to be honest, it's very much a case of business as usual until mid-afternoon, when the place starts to come alive. There are obviously far more people around the ground on days like this, with our match-day staff – people like turnstile operators and stewards and programme sellers – arriving as the afternoon wears on. Many of these people have other jobs, of course, and although we like them to be at Villa Park by 5.30, we make allowances for the fact they have been working somewhere else all day. Usually, we ask them to get to us as early as they can, and it's not often anyone lets us down.

Sometimes, the referee will call into my office for a chat and a cup of tea when he arrives, although this has become more infrequent in recent seasons. At one time refs came in without fail, and I used to love it when Neil Midgley was in charge of our games. We would chat for half an hour or more, and Neil always had a few funny stories to tell. I'm sure it was his great sense of humour which gave him such a good rapport with players, and made him such an excellent referee. It seems to me that the modern game, with all its pressures, has drained football of such characters. One notable exception is Birmingham's Mike Reed who is always willing to have a laugh and a joke on the pitch. Sadly he's never allowed to referee our games – he's a Villa fan.

The time from 4pm until kick-off just flies by. The visiting club's directors usually arrive quite early, followed by the team bus, which is parked in a special area alongside the players' and directors' entrance. To be fair, I don't get involved in welcoming our guests, and my duties on match-day are generally less time-consuming than normal.

Don't get the idea, though, that this means I can put my feet up, or enjoy a meal and a drink with the visiting officials. I'm constantly at the ready in case any problems arise. Just imagine if there was a security alert and the club secretary was too busy wining and dining to deal with it. Thankfully tonight goes without a hitch, but I'm always a little on edge in the build-up to a game.

It seems our players are also on edge during this particular match. Wednesday beat us by a single goal, and coming straight on top of last Saturday's FA Cup defeat at Derby, there are plenty of long faces around the guest lounge afterwards. I'm no exception, although my disappointment at Villa losing a football match is soon put into perspective.

First, I bump into our former assistant manager Jim Barron, whose girlfriend Lauren was killed in a car crash in the early hours of New Year's Day. Jim was badly injured in the crash, so it's good to see him out and about again, but I'm at a loss to know what to say to him. Then Superintendent Colin McDonald, our match-day police commander, taps me on the shoulder and asks me to have a word with the father and brother of Nicola Dixon, a Sutton Coldfield girl who was murdered, also on New Year's Day. Driving home a little later, I'm still depressed about the result, but having just been in close contact with the victims of such tragedies, the fact we have lost seems insignificant.

By the time I'm back home it's around 11.30. Carolyn and the kids are in bed, so I make a cup of coffee and read the paper for half an hour to unwind a little. It's been a 14-hour day, and a miserable one, too. This is one match-day I would prefer to forget.

Thursday, 30 January

There's a beauty parade at Villa Park today, but don't get too excited. We're not being invaded by leggy lovelies, but by pin-striped gentlemen from the business world.

Having decided to go public the club are appointing a Public Relations company to oversee our Stock Market flotation, and three companies have been invited to tender for the job. This, I'm told, is known as a "beauty parade", although it bears no resemblance to the night I was on the judging panel for Miss Iceland.

The directors are joined for the selection process by Chris Hawkley of our stockbrokers Albert E. Sharp, David Owen from Villa's solicitors Edge & Ellison, and Mark Ansell from the club's accountants Deloitte Touche, and we spend hours listening to the presentations of the respective candidates.

Our first meeting starts at 11am, the second at 2pm and the third at 4pm, but the last company turn up late and it's almost three hours later before the whole process is completed. The flotation is a big learning curve for me, but the more I get to know, the more interesting it becomes. I've even started to use the same terminology as people in the City.

In between the presentations, I manage to get back to my office briefly to catch up with correspondence and phone calls, but this is one of those days when the main item on the agenda is anything but routine.

Bringing in a PR company isn't quite like appointing a new

manager or signing a player, but in the overall picture of the club, it's an important decision. Two of the candidates are from Birmingham, but we eventually decide that the most impressive are the London-based Buchanan Communications. Here's hoping they will do the business for us.

FRIDAY, 31 JANUARY

Driving to work this morning, it suddenly crosses my mind that even people who think they know football inside out really have little idea what this job involves. Among the questions I've sometimes been asked is whether it involves typing and shorthand, and whether the job is full-time!

It's certainly seemed full-time this week – plus a bit more besides. Early mornings, late nights, a court appearance, a beauty parade (the wrong kind, unfortunately) and a Premiership home fixture have provided plenty to keep me occupied. I won't mind at all if today follows a more routine pattern, particularly with another home match coming up tomorrow.

Most days, to be fair, are routine, although that can involve anything from players contracts to making sure the club adheres to FA and Premiership rules, from attending league meetings in London to making sure everything is in order in the Ticket Office. The list is endless. At least – unlike club secretaries up until the Second World War – I don't have to pick the team.

Beyond what I would describe as straightforward administrative matters, though, you never know on your way to the ground just what the day might throw at you. One Friday a couple of years ago, for instance, must rank as one of the busiest I have known at Villa Park. We transferred midfielder Garry Parker to Leicester City, we took Franz Carr from Filbert Street as part of the deal, and we were involved in deep negotiations with Jim Barron over the settlement for his sacking as assistant manager two months earlier.

It was also the day Leicester finally withdrew their compensation claim over Brian Little's departure to become our manager. That in itself involved lawyers ringing the ground all day to sort things out. To cap it all, when I managed to get away at around 7pm, I had to go and see John Fashanu. The former Wimbledon striker had suffered a nasty knee injury in a tackle with Manchester United's Ryan Giggs at Old Trafford the previous Saturday, and feared it might end his career.

Fash was as much a businessman as a footballer, and he wanted me to go and see him to discuss the various financial implications in the event of him being forced to retire, which he eventually did later in the year.

To be honest, I was so busy when Fash phoned that I only half listened to the directions he gave me to get to his home in Canwell, just outside Sutton Coldfield. How I wish I'd taken more notice. It was lashing with rain that night, and at one point, having taken a wrong turn, I found myself half a mile along a single dirt track. It wasn't much fun trying to reverse all the way back with no lights to guide me, and my wheels spinning in the mud.

After talking business for half an hour, Fash and I later chatted about the next day's game, at home to his former club Wimbledon. How did he think it would go, I asked. Fash considered the question for a few seconds before declaring it would be a tight game. We won 7-1. So much for his ability to predict the outcome of football matches.

Recollections of that hectic Friday are going through my mind as I pull on to the car park outside the North Stand reception, get out of the car and go in to face another day. Don't they always say that when you are expecting the worst, it doesn't happen? Friday January 31, much to my relief, is a routine day – minus the typing and shorthand.

Saturday, 1 February

Another match day. When the team are away, I usually spend Saturday morning behind the wheel of the car, travelling with the chairman and club doctors David Targett and Barrie Smith, to the opposition ground. But the hours before home fixtures are devoted to tying up any loose ends from the week's work.

In the early days, Saturday mornings were hectic because I used to do everything, but a lot of the load has been taken off my shoulders by stadium manager Ted Small and Safety Operations Manager John Hood. The bank of closed-circuit TV screens in John's control room enable him to keep an eye on turnstiles all around the ground, and ensure that unnecessary congestion is avoided. Despite the sophisticated technology now at our fingertips, though, things can still go wrong. It usually happens when you least expect it, and whatever the problem, the buck stops at my door.

This morning I'm just grateful there will be no repeat of the horror show we experienced at the early-season home match against Arsenal. Our credit card ticket bookings are handled by a London-based agency called Ticketmaster, who send the appropriate tickets to us by courier service on Friday afternoon, for collection by supporters before the game.

For some reason, there was a misunderstanding (a cock-up was possibly a more appropriate description) on the weekend of the Arsenal game, with the courier under the impression it would be okay to deliver the tickets on the Monday.

This, of course, was of precious little use when we were staging a Saturday afternoon Premiership fixture which was almost a sell-out. When the tickets hadn't arrived by 11am on match-day, panic began to set in. We tried to contact the courier company, without success, and although Ticketmaster had a list of all the tickets they had issued, it was clearly going to be a long, tedious business trying to sort everyone out.

Every time someone turned up to collect their credit card tickets, we had to ring Ticketmaster to check names, addresses and seat details before the tickets were re-issued. It was half-time by the time the last of the 200 people affected got into the ground, and understandably, they were far from happy. I missed the first half, too, which is something I had to accept, and I couldn't tell you anything about what happened in the second half either. I just sat there staring into space, annoyed that we had let so many people down. Since then, we have installed a computer link-up from Ticketmaster's offices to Villa Park to ensure it doesn't happen again, but that afternoon still gives me nightmares.

Thankfully, everything goes smoothly ahead of today's match against Sunderland. There's plenty of discussion about our proposed flotation with the directors of Sunderland, who joined the Stock Market just before Christmas, and I also bump into Polish full-back Dariusz Kubicki, one of our former players and now a regular for the Wearsiders.

Kubicki's English has improved beyond recognition since he first came to this country in 1991, and you no longer have to speak deliberately slowly for him. Not that the likes of Dalian Atkinson, Dwight Yorke and our other black players ever did.

I recall one conversation with Dariusz just after he joined us from Legia Warsaw. "I appreciate that you speak slowly for me," he said. "Stuart Gray, my room-mate, also speaks slowly. But the dark boys talk too quickly!"

Sunday, 2 February

Once known as the *Day of Rest*, Sunday has become an integral part of football life. Very often, clubs find themselves in action on the Sabbath because of the demands of television, and I must confess I'm never very keen when Villa have a Sunday game. It usually means working seven days on the trot, which isn't much fun, no matter how much you enjoy your job.

Even if there's no match, it's sometimes difficult to relax, because Sundays at home are frequently disrupted by telephone calls about matters requiring my attention.

Thankfully, this is a phone-free day, and after such a hectic week, I can't say I'm sorry. The biggest decision I have to make is which music to blast through the hi-fi system. Will it be The Beatles or The Byrds, Crowded House or Clapton ? What the hell, with all this time on my hands, I might just play them all.

Chapter Twenty

With A Little Help From My Friends

So there you have it, the life and times of a football club secretary, or what it's been like working for Aston Villa for the past 25 years. There were some worried faces around the ground, I can tell you, when I announced my intention to embark on this project, but hopefully I haven't offended anyone too much. Perhaps I'll write that blockbuster just before I retire and provide myself with a big fat pension!

You've probably noticed that I've resisted naming my all-time Villa team, which is the sort of thing which usually fills a chapter in a book of this nature. The reason, quite frankly, is that I find that kind of thing pretty boring. For one thing, there are numerous books about the club which concentrate on such topics; for another, I don't regard my opinion as any more important than that of anyone sitting in the Trinity Road stand, the Holte End, the Doug Ellis stand or the North stand.

There is, to be honest, a third reason why I haven't gone into detail about the qualities of players. If I were to name my best-ever line-up, I'm afraid my team selection would be heavily influenced by personalities. I would be guilty of letting personal feelings cloud my judgement. A lot of players have become good friends down the years, but that doesn't necessarily mean they would get a place. On the other side of the coin, one international who would possibly have been in my *Top Team* would find himself left out because of an unsavoury incident between the two of us. I don't intend to name him, but we had quite a heated discussion after I wrote to tell him off (politely, I should add) for having his picture taken for a newspaper in a tracksuit advertising one of the rival companies of our kit suppliers.

The following day, he stormed into my office, shouting and swearing, and letting me know what he thought about my letter. I told him to go back outside, calm down, and then come back and conduct the conversation in a civilised manner. In fairness, that's what he did, but the incident still rankles with me, and I certainly wouldn't want to include him in my *Best Villa XI*, if I were ever forced to select one.

Wouldn't make a very good manager, would I? You also have to remember that other players have become close friends, particularly those from the early days, so personalities would get in the way of any selection process. Don't forget that when I joined the club, I was only 21, and younger than most of the first team squad. Now I'm old enough to be the father of virtually the whole of the current squad. Simon Grayson, one of our summer signings, actually shares my birthday. The only problem is, he's 19 years younger.

I've been similarly reluctant to offer a long list of my favourite games, either, other than the 1971 League Cup semi-final victory over Manchester United, but if you really want to twist my arm further on that subject, three other games stand out from the rest, all of them vintage 1994.

For sheer spine-tingling excitement, the Coca-Cola Cup semi-final against Tranmere Rovers must rank as Villa's most gripping encounter of the past two decades. Trailing 3-0 in the first leg at Prenton Park, we looked dead and buried, but Dalian Atkinson's last-gasp goal threw us a lifeline which set the scene for an epic return match at Villa Park. Even then, our prospects still looked bleak when we were still behind on aggregate going into the last few minutes of normal time. But

Atkinson came up with another dramatic effort which took the tie into extra-time. We eventually booked a ticket to Wembley when goal-keeper Mark Bosnich performed heroics during the penalty shoot-out.

A good many supporters, and a few of the players, too, couldn't bear to watch as some of those penalties were being taken. That certainly wasn't the case a month later when we looked on in sheer admiration as the side produced a magnificent Wembley display in the final. Manchester United, who would later win a Premiership and FA Cup double, simply had no answer. In terms of tactical awareness and inventive football, that has to rank as Villa's most satisfying performance of the past two decades. The European Cup triumph may have been a greater achievement, but the final against Bayern Munich never scaled the heights of Wembley 94.

Later that year, to round off a hat-trick of classic contests, we had to endure another nail-biting Villa Park penalty shoot-out. Italian giants Inter Milan beat us 1-0 at the San Siro stadium, Ray Houghton's goal gave us victory by the same margin at home, and then it was down to the lottery of penalties. This time our full-back Phil King held the winning ticket, ramming home the decisive spot kick which ensured our passage to the next round.

I've also had the pleasure of visiting some of the most fabulous sports stadiums in the world during my time with Villa, with Barcelona's Nou Camp and the Pasadena Rose Bowl, two vast, sweeping arenas, standing out above the rest. Not that there was a great deal of atmosphere in Pasadena when we played there during our 1997 summer tour to California.

The 105,000-capacity venue, which had been packed for the World Cup Final between Brazil and Italy three years earlier, had rather an eerie feeling when Los Angeles Galaxy played Aston Villa in a friendly in front of just 8,500 people. Even the fact that Stan Collymore, our £7m record signing, was making his first appearance, failed to create much interest among the locals.

If the Nou Camp and the Rose Bowl are the two most impressive grounds I've visited, however, the most intimidating is unquestionably the lesser-known Inonu Stadium, home of Turkish club Besiktas. It may be less than half the size of those other two giant arenas, but when 45,000 vociferous Turks are crammed in there, the place can be pretty frightening for a visiting team.

I discovered just how passionate these supporters can be when Villa played there in the first round of our 1982-83 European Cup campaign. As holders of the trophy, you would have thought we were used to such fervour in foreign fields, but the atmosphere that night was as hostile as anything I've experienced.

Before the match, I went out with the players to take a look at the playing surface. Like many foreign stadiums, the dressing rooms are under the pitch, and you have to walk down a long corridor before climbing the steps to daylight. As we emerged, it was as if the whole place was about to collapse on our heads as the home fans went through what amounted to a well-rehearsed war-cry from all corners of the ground. Time and again, and getting faster and louder all the while, the chant "Bes-ik-tas-yah!" reverberated around that heaving stadium.

More recently, we have come across similar hostility against another Turkish club, Trabzonspor. The noise level wasn't quite so great as in Besiktas, but it was an infinitely more dangerous situation. When I went to Trabzon to make arrangements for our official party and supporters, I was informed that any coins, pens or other items which might be thrown on the pitch would be confiscated at the turnstiles. This information was duly passed on to our travelling contingent of supporters, but it became apparent that home fans did not have to adhere to such strict regulations.

As we sat there on the night of the match we could hear shots being fired into the air from the terraces. Coins and pens may have been banned, but Trabzonspor presumably had no objection to guns!

It's fair to say that British clubs don't often get a very friendly reception when playing abroad, and sometimes I think we would do better in European competition if our own crowds were equally intimidating towards the opposition.

Off the pitch, though, there's never anything other than a warm welcome for visitors to Villa Park, whether they are officials of opposition clubs or members of the public calling in to buy tickets.

The first point of contact at any club, or any company, for that matter, is the reception area, and you won't find a friendlier welcome anywhere in football than that provided by Marie Priest or Margaret Ward, our two receptionists. Whether they are answering phone calls or dealing with inquiries in person, our front office girls are never less than courteous and helpful.

Marie has been with the club for 17 years, even though she never actually applied for the job. It was her twin sister Sue who wrote asking for employment, but in the meantime she found something else, and it was Marie who turned up for the interview and was subsequently taken on to the staff.

The fact that she has been with us so long is an indication of the family atmosphere at Villa. Most of the staff, in fact, have been with the club for between 15 and 20 years, and there has been little turnover. The great thing about the backroom people is a tremendous sense of loyalty. We have a team behind the scenes who couldn't have any more pride in Aston Villa if they were stepping out to play for the team.

My own secretary Pam Silk has been with the club for two decades, and has worked with me for the majority of that time. Pam came for her interview on the day we played Port Vale in a fifth round FA Cup-tie in February 1977, and made an immediate impression with her friendly, efficient manner, something she has maintained and even improved upon over the years.

Not that I would ever want to put her in charge of transport. At the end of her interview she promptly lost her car keys, and to this day she still has problems some evenings in remembering where she has put them. Pam assists me in making sure I don't forget appointments and dealing with correspondence, while the chairman's personal assistant,

Marion Stringer, also helps out when trickier letters require a response.

Stadium manager Ted Small has devoted the majority of his working life to Villa, and has been responsible for saving the club hundreds of thousands of pounds in the rebuilding of Villa Park. When the Witton Lane stand was transformed into a two-tier structure, for instance, he took control of the project and avoided the need for us to go through the costly business of bringing in outside contractors.

While Ted's engineering talents save money in one direction, Abdul Rashid's commercial know-how makes us a small fortune even when there's no match to generate revenue. Abdul has risen from a Villa ball-boy to hold the important position of head of a department which brings in millions of pounds every year – more, in fact, than our gate receipts.

The club shop, managed by Alan Williams, has also expanded rapidly in recent years, to the point where we now have what amounts to a superstore, the Villa Village, which is one of the biggest of its kind in the country. This new complex is the domain of John Greenfield, who was formerly our promotions manager, and now carries the title Merchandising Manager.

John may be pretty hot when it comes to selling, but he was well and truly hooked when I decided to play a practical joke on him a couple of years ago. The Villa magazine, *Claret & Blue*, had run a story, complete with pictures and graphics, explaining that because the stadium was originally built on a filled-in pond, there was a danger of water levels rising and the pitch subsiding. The story went on to say that while remedial work was being carried out to prevent flooding, we would have to ground-share with neighbours Birmingham City and West Bromwich Albion. Abdul Rashid was even quoted as suggesting that as a thank-you gesture to Blues, we would dig up our pitch and replant it at St Andrew's, where they were having problems with their playing surface.

Most of the Villa staff realised that the whole story was no more than an elaborate *April Fool*, but when John got wind of it, he came into my office with a worried expression, to check if it were true. I told him we'd even received a government document outlining the problem in detail, but I couldn't show it him because Marion Stringer had it. While he was walking down the corridor to investigate further, I rang Marion and asked her to keep John guessing. She, in turn, said she couldn't let him see the document because it was now in the hands of the chairman, who was furious about all the money this water problem was going to cost. It was only while returning to his office that John suddenly realised what day it was.

That incident highlights the camaraderie we have at Villa Park. There's a job to be done, and everyone does it to the best of their ability, but there's always time for a laugh and a joke when the occasion presents itself. Basically, we're one happy family (quite a large one these days, too) and that plays an important part in keeping the operation running smoothly. I certainly wouldn't have it any other way. The past 25 years have been enjoyable, quite apart from Villa's achievements on the football pitch, because of the people I've worked with. As the Beatles might say, I get by with a little help from my friends.

In tune with Kent Neilsen and Jeff Lynne.